Praise for *Growing Up Mindful*

"A wonderful, practical book for kids and adults that is reassuring, accessible, and enjoyable. Chock-full of useful and engaging practices, it is a great resource for parents, therapists, and teachers. Chris Willard is a rising star whose attunement to the needs of children shines through on every page."

SUSAN M. POLLAK
President, Institute for Meditation and
Psychotherapy, coauthor of *Sitting Together*

"A wonderful approach to learning mindfulness—full of great skills, practical tools, and enormously helpful wisdom."

JACK KORNFIELD
author of *The Wise Heart*

"*Growing up Mindful* is filled with wisdom and expert guidance in sharing the blessings of mindfulness with young people. Drawing on his vast experience as teacher, clinician and practitioner, Chris Willard provides the kind of practical, doable exercises and reflections that will help you bring mindfulness alive in all the situations of daily life."

TARA BRACH, PHD
author of *Radical Acceptance* and *True Refuge*

"As the benefits of mindfulness become well established, a recurring question is, 'How do you teach this stuff to kids?' Look no further. This book is a treasure trove of exercises and practical wisdom to inspire any reader. The author's playful approach leaves us with the understanding that anyone can become more mindful and still be who we are. May we all practice like this, starting with the kids or with our own inner child."

CHRISTOPHER GERMER, PHD
author of *The Mindful Path to Self-Compassion*; co-editor,
Mindfulness and Psychotherapy; faculty, Harvard Medical School

"Chris Willard's new book *Growing Up Mindful* is jam-packed with great advice and practices for children, teens, and families. It is a wonderful resource for parents, therapists, and teachers worldwide!"

SUSAN KAISER GREENLAND
author of *The Mindful Child* and cofounder of Inner Kids

"Many of the deepest experiences youth have with mindfulness do not happen in formal, structured lessons. They happen in the 'micro-moments' of daily life. With a variety of short, conceptually simple methods, *Growing Up Mindful* is one of the few mindfulness and youth books that is structured to reflect this truth. If you are looking for developmentally appropriate ways to introduce practice to youth in a way that will stick, this is your book."

CHRIS MCKENNA
Program Director, Mindful Schools (mindfulschools.org)

"Practical, engaging, and a pleasure to read, this inspirational book is an invaluable resource for parents, teachers, and anyone else who works with or cares for kids. Based on extensive experience, it's chock-full of creative, common-sense practices that can help virtually any child, adolescent, or adult live a happier, richer, more engaged, life."

RONALD D. SIEGEL, PSYD
author of *The Mindfulness Solution: Everyday Practices for Everyday Problems*; assistant professor of psychology, Harvard Medical School

"This book offers a wonderful array of simple, playful, engaging mindfulness practices which can be shared by parents, teachers, and therapists with children at home, at school, and in clinical settings. Dr. Willard has created an invaluable resource to support you in sharing the nourishing power of mindfulness with children and adolescents. Like your go-to cookbook, this book is filled with healthy, delicious, satisfying mindfulness recipes that you can prepare and savor with the young people in your life."

AMY SALTZMAN, MD
author of *A Still Quiet Place: A Mindfulness Program for Teaching Children and Adolescents to Ease Stress and Difficult Emotions* and *A Still Quiet Place for Teens: A Mindfulness Workbook to Ease Stress and Difficult Emotions*

"Whether you're a mindfulness newbie or a mindfulness instructor, in Chris Willard's *Growing up Mindful* you'll find wise answers to questions about sharing mindfulness that you have now and that you'll have in the future. This book is a gift—for yourself, for a friend, for a teacher."

RICHARD BRADY
founder, Mindfulness in Education Network

"This is a splendid and timely book, the richness and accessibility of which will be of enormous support to children and young people and those who live and work with them—and in particular to parents, a group very much on the front line in experiencing the fallout from teenage stress, but who have so far been lacking much guidance in the vital coping skills of mindfulness. It is an inspiring beginner's guide written by one of the best-respected practitioners in the field with a deep store of personal knowledge of what works in engaging young people in mindfulness, as well as a convincing grasp of the scientific evidence base. The style is friendly, pacey, fun, and approachable; the use of vivid anecdotes keeps it real; and the practices combine authenticity and practicality for fitting into the busy lives of families and young people—some are only a minute long. I will be using it myself to help with my parenting skills, and will recommend it widely."

KATHERINE WEARE
Emeritus Professor, School of Education, University of Southampton, UK

growing
up
mindful

Also by Christopher Willard, PsyD

BOOKS

The Mindfulness and Depression Workbook for Teens,
coauthored with Mitch Abblett, PhD

Mindfulness with Youth: From the Classroom to the Clinic,
coedited with Amy Saltzman, MD

The Mindfulness and Anxiety Workbook for Teens

*Child's Mind: Mindfulness Practices to Help Our Children
Be More Focused, Calm, and Relaxed*

AUDIO

*Practices for Growing Up Mindful: Guided Meditations
and Simple Exercises for Children, Teens, and Families*

CARDS

The Growing Mindful Deck,
coauthored with Mitch Abblett, PhD

growing up mindful

ESSENTIAL PRACTICES TO HELP
CHILDREN, TEENS, AND FAMILIES FIND
BALANCE, CALM, AND RESILIENCE

CHRISTOPHER WILLARD, PSYD

sounds true
BOULDER, COLORADO

Sounds True
Boulder, CO 80306

This work is solely for personal growth and education. It should not be treated as a
substitute for professional assistance, therapeutic activities such as psychotherapy
or counseling, or medical advice. In the event of physical or mental distress, please
consult with appropriate health professionals. The application of protocols and
information in this book is the choice of each reader, who assumes full responsibility for his or her understandings, interpretations, and results. The author and
publisher assume no responsibility for the actions or choices of any reader.

Cover design by Rachael Murray
Book design by Beth Skelley

Printed in Canada

Excerpt on pages 99–100 reprinted from *Interbeing: Fourteen Guidelines for
Engaged Buddhism* (1998) by Thich Nhat Hanh with permission of Parallax Press,
Berkeley, California, www.parallax.org.

Excerpt on pages 140-41 reprinted from *Being Peace* (rev. ed. 2005) by Thich Nhat
Hanh with permission of Parallax Press, Berkeley, California, www.parallax.org.

Library of Congress Cataloging-in-Publication Data
Willard, Christopher (Psychologist)
  Growing up mindful : essential practices to help children, teens,
and families find balance, calm, and resilience / Christopher Willard, PsyD.
    pages cm
Includes bibliographical references.
ISBN 978-1-62203-590-8
1. Meditation for children. 2. Meditation—Therapeutic use.
3. Mindfulness (Psychology) I. Title.
BF723.M37W554 2016
158.1ʾ2—dc23
                          2015034114

Ebook ISBN 978-1-62203-631-8

10 9 8 7 6 5 4 3 2 1

For Leo

There can be no keener revelation of a society's soul

than the way in which it treats its children.

NELSON MANDELA

opening words of his speech at the launch of the Nelson
Mandela Children's Fund in Pretoria, South Africa, May 1995

contents

preface

By picking up this book, you are embarking on something incredible and world-changing. And wherever you are and whatever you might be feeling, you are not alone. You are joining the growing movement to bring wonder, curiosity, and reflection back into childhood, from which they have been slowly disappearing. This book and others like it exist because there is an audience, a community of others who, like you, want to help the next generation live more fully and compassionately. A Chinese proverb says, "One generation plants the seeds; the next enjoys the shade." It starts with you; it starts with us. So whether you are a parent or a professional, thank you. I am honored to be a part of this journey with you and others who are quietly planting and watering the seeds of mindfulness in their communities.

introduction

Meditation is a microcosm, a model, and a mirror. The skills we practice when we sit are transferable to the rest of our lives.

SHARON SALZBERG, *Real Happiness*

∪

Mindfulness with kids doesn't have to mean twenty minutes of quietly sitting on a meditation cushion. In my time as a teacher, therapist, and parent, I've seen hundreds of kids of all ages and backgrounds practice mindfulness, and each kid's mindfulness practice looks as different as the kids themselves.

For seven-year-old Jackie, who struggles with ADHD and divorcing parents, it means playing with stuffed animals on the floor until either she or I ring a bell, and then we both take three mindful breaths. With Alexa, a curly-haired teen who struggles with food, mindfulness means tuning in to her body's signals, so she can respond to what her body, not her emotions, tells her she needs to eat. For burly Jared, an athlete who fears panicking on the lacrosse field, it means doing a quick body scan during a game and bringing his awareness to the soles of his feet when he senses his anxiety rising. For Ellie, who first came to my office at age twelve for chronic pain related to a childhood illness, it means sitting quietly on a cushion with the meditation club at school and trying her first teen mindfulness retreat for her own spiritual development.

For a classroom teacher, mindfulness might mean offering kids a focused listening practice to do before state exams; for a therapist, it might mean having the client draw while engaging all of their senses in the process. For me, until my son was born, it meant meditation retreats and Wednesdays at a meditation center. Now it means noticing my joys and fears about his future and the world he will enter arise as I watch him at rest or at play.

No matter how we practice it, mindfulness offers the gift of calm and clarity when difficult times arise, which they inevitably will, no matter how hard we try to protect our children. The world is not always a compassionate place; they will get hurt, if they haven't been already. But if we teach them, they can discover that their greatest challenges can be the greatest teachers. One of the gifts of mindfulness is that it transforms life's inevitable pain into wisdom and compassion. The great philosophers all speak of pain as the touchstone of spiritual growth. If we want our kids to grow and flourish rather than be stunted by life's challenges, we must offer them the tools to work with suffering.

Human beings need to experience some degree of pain in order to develop compassion, and life is guaranteed to give it to us. Contemplative practices like mindfulness allow kids to heal and soothe themselves rather than distract themselves from the pain. Kids need to get hurt, scrape their knees, bomb the occasional test, cry over their first heartbreak, and see that they can survive and grow from the experience. And when they share their experience with others, they too can alleviate suffering in the world.

Although many people associate mindfulness with Buddhism, you don't have to be Buddhist, religious, or even spiritual to practice mindfulness or appreciate how it can help us all, personally and collectively. The story of the historical Buddha is essentially the tale of an overprotected child, with high-powered helicopter parents who outsourced their parenting to keep their child protected, sheltered, and safe so that he would be prepared for a stable, predictable adulthood. It was only when the young man encountered suffering in the world that he began a lifelong quest to end suffering, which he found through wisdom and compassion practices. Jesus transformed his suffering into salvation for all humanity. Judaism seeks to transform the suffering of a people into finding meaning and healing a wounded world. Other religions and philosophies seek to transform and transcend earthly challenges.

The psychological research on mindfulness shows that it greatly enhances what psychologists call "flourishing"—the opposite of depression, avoidance, and disengagement. Mindfulness builds emotional intelligence, boosts happiness, increases curiosity and engagement, reduces anxiety, soothes difficult emotions and trauma, and helps kids (and adults) focus, learn, and make better choices.

In our distracted world, the default reaction to stress, unpleasant experiences, or even just neutral experiences is to *check out*. Don't like how you feel inside? Bored with where you are in the present moment? Check out with something outside of yourself—watch a video, play a game, check your Twitter feed, scroll through Instagram. A recent study found that young men would rather receive ten minutes of low-level electric shocks than spend ten minutes alone with their thoughts, without their electronics.[1] Taking drugs, cutting themselves, and acting out are other ways kids check out of their immediate experience. When we teach children to disconnect from their experience from a young age, it's no wonder they struggle with their emotions.

Mindfulness and compassion practices go radically against this cultural conditioning by emphasizing *checking in*—with our experience, with ourselves, and with the world around us—rather than *checking out*. Over time, kids learn to tolerate their experiences, whether they are comfortable or not, and come to see that everything in the range of human experience, pleasant or unpleasant, loved or loathed, eventually passes. Over time, through the lens of mindfulness, they may even become curious about their experience, their triggers, and their automatic responses. Teaching children to check in with, rather than check out of, their experience builds emotional intelligence, leading to happier kids and families. And the benefits can go viral through communities, leading to happier classrooms, schools, hospitals, and mental health clinics—and ultimately, to a happier, more compassionate future for humanity.

In fact, some of the most exciting research in mindfulness shows that these practices are helpful not only for the kids in your life. They can also help *you* be calmer, less burned out, less reactive, more present, and more effective as a parent or partner or professional. This is one of the most precious gifts of mindfulness practice: that what we practice ourselves, physically, emotionally, spiritually, personally, and professionally, helps others.

About This Book

In working with young people over the last few decades, I've discovered that mindfulness can be learned by anyone, from young children with significant disabilities to rebellious adolescents. I have seen that they all can practice and all can benefit from even a small dose of mindfulness. That's why this book contains more than seventy practices—so that you can find at least a few that work for you and your kids. Each one has been road-tested by me, other parents, therapists, teachers, and, most importantly, by actual kids. What's more, you don't have to be an expert. Simple practices can be shared with kids by anyone with an authentic and openhearted intention.

The last thing I want to do is to make mindfulness another chore or something to add to the overbooked lives of families and teachers. For that reason, chapter 11 includes dozens of practices that take less than a minute. This book also includes ways to bring mindfulness to what you and your kids are already doing, including eating, walking, playing sports, making art, and even using technology.

This book does not offer a curriculum, but rather a set of building blocks and instructions for sharing mindfulness with kids at their pace, for their minds. When I was a kid, my favorite toy was LEGO, because I could get a set and build it according to the instructions or, if I wanted, make my own creation from the same blocks. My hope is that you will play with the practices in this book to create something together with your kids.

Part I covers the basics of mindfulness, while touching on the theory, research, and science behind it. Whether mindfulness is brand-new to you or a subject you already know a great deal about, having a solid foundation in why mindfulness matters is important when we share mindfulness with kids or with other adults. Chapter 3 covers practices for you, the adult, because sharing mindfulness starts with your own practice.

Part II delves into a variety of practices, and offers adaptations for the different kinds of kids in the world and the different places they go—family, school, and elsewhere. We will talk about classroom adaptations, group adaptations, and age and learning-style adaptations.

Part III discusses teaching mindfulness practices in formal settings, getting kids engaged, and ways to create a culture of mindfulness among adults in your community.

The basic mindfulness practices shared in this book have evolved over thousands of years. Until recently, meditation practices were rarely practiced by laypeople, even in places we tend to associate with meditation. Many of the techniques in this book are adaptations of existing practices, often developed by other leaders in mindfulness education, including Susan Kaiser Greenland, Amy Saltzman, Jon Kabat-Zinn, and Thich Nhat Hanh. Some practices originate in spiritual traditions, but all of the practices in this book are secular. Throughout, I have tried to acknowledge the source of the practice as I know it, but this is a challenge in what remains a largely oral tradition.

It is also my intention that this book not be an explanation, but an exploration of mindfulness. I invite you to experience the transformative power of mindfulness for yourself and for the kids in your life. Learn or deepen your knowledge of the practices, and share the ones that resonate with you. Suspend judgment and open your mind and heart, letting go of preconceptions and prejudgments about some of the activities, and give them a try, doing the practices as you read. Let this book be a lab manual, and you both the guinea pig and the scientist.

Experiment with all the practices in this book, even if they don't seem like your thing. Some will resonate for you; some won't. I encourage you to be a little bit brave and a little bit vulnerable, and to let go of the self-consciousness we adults have developed. Being vulnerable and taking risks is what we ask our children to do on a regular basis—at the dinner table when we ask them to try a new vegetable, in the classroom when we teach them a new math concept, or in the therapy office when we ask them to share deeply personal stories. To connect authentically with them, we need to experience and model the same vulnerability we ask of them. If we expect our children to be open to new experiences, it's only fair that we are too. So move your body in new ways to uncover new awareness, color if you've not picked up a crayon in decades, sing even if you hate the sound of your voice, and create something new to share. Most importantly, *have fun.*

As you read and try the practices, allow yourself to be surprised by what resonates for you and what doesn't. Try a little bit of everything your first time through this book, then return to pick out what works for you and your kids.

Thich Nhat Hanh, the Vietnamese monk known, perhaps more than anyone else, for bringing mindfulness to the West, uses the metaphor of planting seeds when he speaks about teaching young people mindfulness and compassion practices. A small seed of mindfulness can be planted in anyone, and it is capable of growing and blossoming into a mindful, caring life. This book will help you not only plant the seeds, but also create the conditions under which young people can flourish and bloom—physically, emotionally, intellectually, and spiritually.

PART I

understanding mindfulness

CHAPTER 1

stress and the american kid

Life moves pretty fast. If you don't stop and look
around once in a while, you could miss it.

FERRIS BUELLER, in *Ferris Bueller's Day Off*

∪

In 2014, the American Psychological Association did a study of stress in American life. They found that the most stressed group in America are teenagers. If you've spent time with a teenager lately, they could have told you that—or maybe they already did.

Figure 1 shows a Venn diagram making the rounds online. "The Student Paradox" is funny, to be sure, but it's all too relatable for most teens. And this diagram doesn't include other issues, such as caring for a sick parent, dealing with a brother in prison, working an extra job to help keep your parents' house out of foreclosure, and other stresses that many teens are under.

It's not just teens who are under stress. Whether I am speaking to kids in the inner city or students on manicured university campuses, the concerns I hear are the same. Kids of all ages worry about whether they will have a future, given the wars and environmental devastation affecting the planet. They worry about the economy, violence, poverty, and prejudice. It's heartbreaking to hear a slender seven-year-old girl in the suburbs tell me she is too fat to have friends, or an eleven-year-old boy in the city tell me the only way he will live past twenty is if he's in jail. No matter what background a kid is from, suffering and fear are universal.

Not only are kids under more stress, but they also have fewer skills for coping with it. Overburdened parents and teachers don't know how to help; schools are cutting life skills programs to make room for high-stakes testing. Yet if young people don't learn to manage stress by the time they hit their teenage years, they are hardly likely to learn later. Automatic responses to stress are learned at an early age and reinforced by life experiences. Stress, and kids' responses to it, are contagious, spreading from kid to kid and through schools and families like this year's flu, leading to long- and short-term negative effects on physical health, mental health, and learning. The good news is that mindfulness and compassion are contagious as well.

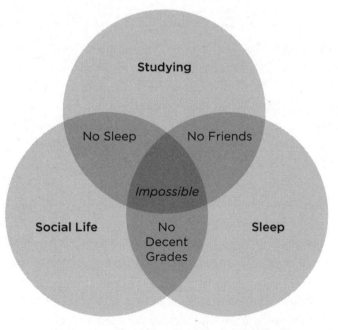

FIGURE 1 The Student Paradox: pick two

How We Usually Respond to Stress

Fundamentally, stress is a response to fear, real or perceived. Humans are hardwired to respond to fear in just a few ways. Our children facing SATs today react in much the same way that our ancestors did when facing a saber-toothed cat. Unfortunately, we haven't evolved that much.

The following exercise, adapted from one taught by Mindful Self-Compassion teachers Christopher Germer and Kristin Neff, demonstrates two of the body's built-in responses to stress.

Close your eyes and hold your hands in front of you, making tight fists. As you do, ask yourself these questions:

- What do you notice in your body? In your mind?
- What kinds of emotions are you feeling?
- What kinds of thoughts are you having?
- When during the day or during the week do you tend to feel this way?
- How does your breath feel right now?
- How open or closed do you feel?
- How energetic do you feel?
- How would it be to feel like this all of the time?

Now release your fists and drop your hands. Slump over and slouch, your head falling toward your chest.

- What do you notice in your body? In your mind?
- What kinds of emotions are you feeling?
- What kinds of thoughts are you having?
- When during the day or during the week do you tend to feel this way?
- How does your breath feel right now?
- How open or closed do you feel?
- How energetic do you feel?
- How would it be to feel like this all of the time?

The first position, making fists, turns on the *fight-or-flight* response to stress, which helps us either fight off what's stressing us out or run away from it. We tend to feel this way in traffic, on that busy day when we open our email to twenty new urgent messages, when our phone starts ringing, and when our child just vomited on the floor as the dog starts barking.

When we're in fight-or-flight mode, our breath is constricted. In fact, our whole body is constricted, along with our mind and heart. It might feel that the slightest thing will set us off—probably because it will. We are on guard, closed off to everything except signals of danger. In our brain, the part called the amygdala (sometimes described as the "reptilian brain," "caveman brain," or "Incredible Hulk brain") is flaring up, while the prefrontal cortex, where we do our best thinking, is shut down. We are thinking only about ourselves and the next few seconds; we are not thinking about the big picture, let alone experiencing compassion or the perspective of others. When we are in this mode, our filters only let in signs of danger, and they interpret even neutral or safe stimuli, such as a helpful parent or teacher, as threats or dangers. Cortisol, the stress hormone, is coursing through us, blocking the brain receptors for oxytocin, the hormone that allows us to feel love, compassion, and other cuddly emotions. The fact that fight-or-flight blocks our compassion explains why we're not willing to lose three seconds by letting someone merge when we're in terrible traffic, or why we snap at our partner or kids after a tough day at work. It perhaps also explains something about bullying and violence in high-stress schools. The body and brain are sending the message that everything is a threat, and there is no room in our response for compassion or understanding.

Many kids spend much of their waking life in fight-or-flight mode, their bodies reacting to danger even when there isn't any. Many describe the fight-or-flight posture as powerful, but its power isn't sustainable. The fight, or attack, response appears as aggression. The flight, or avoid, response manifests as anxiety. The long-term effects of a sustained flight-or-flight stress response are devastating to both mental and physical health, affecting everything from mood and the ability to think clearly, to cardiovascular health, immune functioning (after all, who needs long-term immunity for short-term survival?), and metabolism (yes, all this stress is partly to blame for the obesity crisis), to our relationships.

Too much time in fight-or-flight can cause kids' brains to become rewired for reactivity, making it hard for them to access their own wisdom or think clearly. Parents and teachers may see kids spend hours studying and filling their brains with information, or therapists may help them build a strong set of coping skills, but the kids can still bomb a test or lose their cool in the important moment because they don't have the bandwidth to access their prefrontal cortex or their best self in the moment that counts.

Let's consider the second position, which demonstrates another built-in stress response. The slumped-over position represents the *freeze/submit* response to stress or danger, which gets less press than fight-or-flight. In the modern adult world, we might call this response the four-o'clock-on-a-Friday feeling. Animals in the wild sometimes respond this way to threats; they freeze, hoping to blend in with their surroundings so predators won't see them, or they play dead, hoping to fool predators into leaving them alone. When this response is pervasive, behavioral scientists call it learned helplessness or even depression, which is another reaction to chronic stress or chronic trauma. Behaviorally, it manifests as giving up, turning inward, and shutting out the world. We might all call it the "f– it" response, and see it in ourselves, or in those kids who slump in the back row, appearing to have given up. In the freeze/submit state, too, signals of safety are filtered out, and reasons to give up are filtered in, reinforcing the depressive cycle.

While the freeze/submit response has its advantages and can even feel good, like fight-or-flight it is unsustainable. Giving up is no way to approach an athletic competition or a college interview, and repeated over time it leads further into depression and avoidance.

Both the fight-or-flight and freeze/submit responses have evolved to work well for the physical dangers that our hunter-gatherer ancestors faced, but are ineffective in the face of the emotional dangers and emotional stresses that the modern world presents, where the threats are less to ourselves than to our self-concepts. We don't entirely understand why some people react with aggression, some with anxiety, and some with depression. It may be due to our brain's neural wiring. It may also be due to a combination of genetics, cultural conditioning, and early attachment (or lack of) to caregivers.

The previous exercise with your hands allows you to experience the way a child, or an adult, responding to stress perceives and interacts with the world. The fight response probably looks familiar to anyone who has spent time with an angry child. The flight response belongs to what we might call an anxious child, and the freeze response to a depressed or traumatized child.

Cultivating Skillful Responses to Stress

The good news is that fight, flight, and freeze/submit are not our only options when responding to fear and stress. Today, biologists are studying two other responses to stress built into our bodies and mind. Because we tend not to cultivate these responses in ourselves, many of us rarely experience them.

To show you what I mean, let's return to our demonstration exercise.

Sit or stand up, holding your body not too tightly, not too loosely. Extend your hands out in front of you, palms up and open.
- What do you notice in your body? In your mind?
- What kinds of emotions are you feeling?
- What kinds of thoughts are you having?
- When during the day or during the week do you tend to feel this way?
- How does your breath feel right now?
- How open or closed do you feel?
- How energetic do you feel?
- How would it be to feel like this more of the time?

While still upright, place one or both hands over your heart. Feel the warmth of your hand(s).

- What do you notice in your body? In your mind?
- What kinds of emotions are you feeling?
- What kinds of thoughts are you having?
- When during the day or during the week do you tend to feel this way?
- How does your breath feel right now?
- How open or closed do you feel?
- How energetic do you feel?
- How would it be to feel like this more of the time?

The position with hands up and out represents a stress response called *attending*. This is a qualitatively different stance than fighting, fleeing, or freezing. It is attending to what is actually here. In this stance, we are likely to feel open, awake, and alert, yet calm. We are settled without being sluggish. Rather than avoiding, we face directly whatever is in front of us, whether we like it or not, and we maintain a clear and receptive mind. We might think of this attentive state of body and brain as mindfulness.

When in this mindful, attending response, we can think fully and creatively, using all of our brain. We can focus on both the big picture and what's right in front of us. We can breathe easily and deeply, and as we do, we take in accurate information about the world around us and inside of us. In the brain, the prefrontal lobes are back online, and the amygdala, the internal alarm system, is calm, without stress hormones jamming up the system. In the attend response, we are not passive, but alert and awake.

The last position, with one or both hands over the heart, recreates the *befriend* response. We can think of it as compassion and self-compassion. Not only are we staying present for the stress, for what is difficult for us in the moment, but we are also actively caring for ourselves in that moment and, in the process, learning to befriend the difficult emotions we are having. We can all begin to learn from our emotions, our inner voices, and care for them properly. In the process, we begin caring for ourselves and, in turn, caring for those around us.

You might take a moment to reflect: which of these responses are the best mental state for your kids (or yourself) to be in as they negotiate a new curfew, head into an exam, or approach another potentially stressful situation? The attend and befriend responses are healthier and more sustainable than fight, flight, or freeze/submit, and these too are hardwired into our neural systems. For example, in 2013, I was teaching in Europe when I got news of bombs exploding near the finish line of the Boston Marathon, in my hometown. My first instinctive reaction was to grab my heart, an unconscious, automatic gesture of self-compassion. So it's not that one is better, it's that some are better for certain contexts. So why do we usually default to fight, flight, or freeze/submit responses? Because we haven't cultivated our natural attend and befriend responses or reinforced them when they occur.

That is where mindfulness practice comes in. Using practices that open us up, as in the second part of this exercise, we cultivate new types of awareness and, in doing so, retrain our brains to give us the option of responding to stress with attending and befriending, instead of automatically defaulting to the limiting and draining responses of fight, flight, and freeze/submit. We can also use these practices to help our kids cultivate their attend and befriend responses, so they can find the feelings of open, calm alertness and compassion for themselves when they need it most. Running through this four-position exercise is a good introduction to mindfulness; giving kids or adults the experience of mindfulness through position three will always be more powerful than defining it for them.

When I use this exercise with younger kids, I joke that in the first two positions we are acting and moving like a robot or a rag doll, and in the second two positions we are acting like human beings. Another friend describes these as tiger energy, sloth energy, and swan energy. You or your kids can also playfully say to yourself in fight-or-flight, "I'm calm," or when slumped over, "I can do it!", or in the attend position, "I'm so stressed out," or in the befriend position, "I'm a complete failure." It's almost comical how wrong the words feel.

It's not that stress is bad. We just need to better match our responses to the situations we find ourselves in. Attending and befriending are not the best responses all the time; sometimes we and our kids deal with real danger, and to survive we need to respond by fighting, fleeing (as when a car darts out in front of us), or "freezing" and just vegging out. At first, the attend and befriend responses may make us feel vulnerable, and some kids may not be physically or emotionally safe if they respond in these ways in their neighborhoods or homes. Had I been at the finish line of the Boston marathon when the bomb went off, I would have wanted to be in fight/flight until I reached safety, where I could shift into attend/befriend for myself and others. As adults, we can help kids find spaces where it is safe to practice the attend and befriend responses, so they can kick in when appropriate.

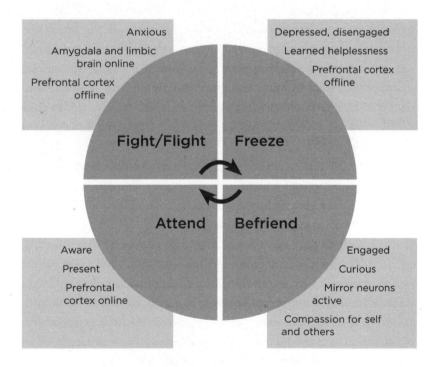

FIGURE 2   Ways we can respond to stress

Mindfulness and the Brain

We used to think that the brain we were born with was the one we were stuck with, once it finished growing in our late teen years. But in the last decade, research on *neuroplasticity*—the ability of our brain to change and grow, like a muscle, as a result of our actions and thoughts—tells a different story.

The brain is a lot like the body. We are born with a set of physical parameters, but if we eat right, take care of ourselves, and work out, we can build muscle, flexibility, and endurance. We can also change the shape and size of our brain, boosting concentration, flexibility, and intelligence and building new neural pathways and networks, by working out our brain, particularly with mindfulness and related practices.

My friend and colleague Sara Lazar, a neuroscientist at Harvard Medical School, has received a lot of attention for scanning the brains of mindfulness meditators with fMRI machines. Her research found exactly that—just as with physical exercise, areas of the brain that are active during mindfulness meditation actually grow with practice.[1]

The main area where growth occurs is in the prefrontal cortex, the area located right behind the forehead. This region is home to our executive functioning; it is the command and control center, where analytical thinking takes place. Here we see the future, understand consequences, see possibilities, and construct plans and strategies to achieve our goals.

This part of the brain also allows us to suppress impulses and not act on every emotion. Attention regulation and what psychologists call working memory live here, keeping us focused and on task, holding information on our cognitive desktop. Many interactions between emotion and thought occur here, as we make sense of emotional signals, then form moral and rational decisions.

Low activity and smaller size of the prefrontal cortex is correlated with psychological conditions such as attention deficit hyperactivity disorder (ADHD), substance abuse and other problematic behaviors, impulse control problems, schizophrenia, distraction, depression, and mood disorders.

Interestingly, this was the last area of the human brain to evolve. You could say that the prefrontal cortex is what makes us human. It is also the last area to develop over our lifespan, reaching full development only in our mid-twenties. Research now suggests that, in males, it isn't fully developed until the late twenties. (Insurance and car rental companies, not to mention parents and teachers and anyone who tried to date in their twenties, figured this out long before scientists.) Research on mindfulness has found improvements in sustained attention (listening to the teacher for the entire class) and selective attention (ignore the spitball flying past), both of which take place in the prefrontal cortex.

The insular cortex, located deeper in the brain, is also active during meditation and grows through regular practice. This region controls visceral processes, including regulating our heart rate, breathing, and hunger. The insular cortex also assists with emotional regulation, the integration of thoughts and emotions, and awareness and self-awareness. Mirror neurons, which give us the ability to put ourselves in another person's shoes and have compassion for them, are located here. This area is often smaller in people with severe mental illness, including bipolar disorder and schizophrenia, yet it appears to get larger with even short-term meditation. Just as our muscles are active during physical workouts, these areas are active during mental workouts and get bigger with repeated use.

A few other brain regions also show positive changes with mindfulness meditation. Researchers believe the temporoparietal junction houses many aspects of emotional intelligence, including the abilities to see situations in a larger perspective, to see the perspective of others, and to consider the larger consequences of actions and behaviors. The hippocampus is important in memory and learning, both learning in the classroom and learning from past behavior. This part of the brain is smaller in patients with post-traumatic stress disorder (PTSD) and in people who struggle socially. The hippocampus helps us respond appropriately to a situation by getting information from the prefrontal cortex, which will help us to choose the wisest action. The posterior cingulate region, which allows us to shift from a self-centered perspective to the big picture, is also changed through mindfulness meditation practice. Other research has found that mindfulness meditation alters

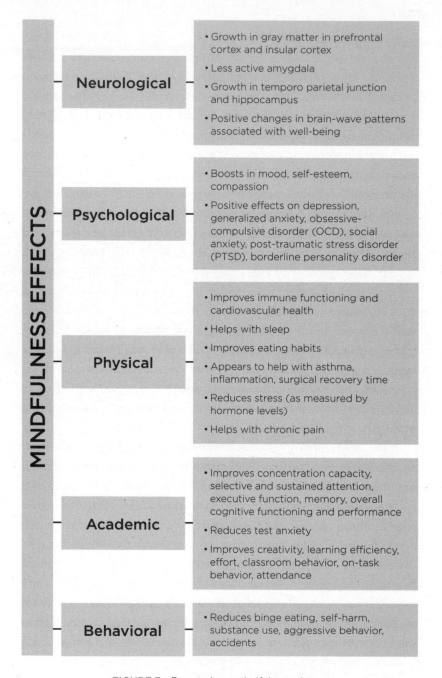

MINDFULNESS EFFECTS

Neurological
- Growth in gray matter in prefrontal cortex and insular cortex
- Less active amygdala
- Growth in temporo parietal junction and hippocampus
- Positive changes in brain-wave patterns associated with well-being

Psychological
- Boosts in mood, self-esteem, compassion
- Positive effects on depression, generalized anxiety, obsessive-compulsive disorder (OCD), social anxiety, post-traumatic stress disorder (PTSD), borderline personality disorder

Physical
- Improves immune functioning and cardiovascular health
- Helps with sleep
- Improves eating habits
- Appears to help with asthma, inflammation, surgical recovery time
- Reduces stress (as measured by hormone levels)
- Helps with chronic pain

Academic
- Improves concentration capacity, selective and sustained attention, executive function, memory, overall cognitive functioning and performance
- Reduces test anxiety
- Improves creativity, learning efficiency, effort, classroom behavior, on-task behavior, attendance

Behavioral
- Reduces binge eating, self-harm, substance use, aggressive behavior, accidents

FIGURE 3 Research on mindfulness shows that it has a variety of positive effects.[2]

our brain-wave patterns in the short and long term to patterns associated with greater happiness.

While some parts of the brain become bigger, stronger, and more active with meditation, other parts of the brain get quieter. One significant change happens in the amygdala, the region most commonly associated with the fight-or-flight and freeze/submit responses to stress, as well as with depression. When the amygdala (caveman brain) is active, the prefrontal cortex (the civilized brain) shuts down, and vice versa. As described earlier, when the amygdala is active, we see threats everywhere and can't think clearly. As it calms down or shrinks, our perspective of danger becomes more realistic, our levels of stress decline, and we can respond rationally rather than react irrationally to stressful events.

The research on mindfulness is well established and growing all the time, from a few dozen studies a year just a decade ago to a few thousand studies in recent years. Figure 3 summarizes what some of the recent research on mindfulness tells about the effects mindfulness can have.

Kids' Brains and Mindfulness Practice

While the brain is always "plastic," or changeable, it is most plastic during childhood. Because children's brains are still developing, they can learn, adapt, and change faster than the brains of adults. (Don't worry, the research shows that it's possible to change your brain and make it calmer, more focused, and less reactive at any age—so you can teach an old dog new tricks!) We can set kids on a course of healthy brain development across their lives through early mindfulness practice.

Consider the less happy times in your own home, the children in your classroom that have a tendency to get under your skin, the types of referral questions that you get in your therapy office. When I ask this question at workshops, I hear the same responses over and over again: *Moodiness. Impulsivity. Unhappiness. Aggression. Self-centeredness. Lack of perspective. Failure to see consequences. Questionable judgment. Mood swings. Emotional thinking. Short attention span. Poor planning.*

Reactivity. Executive functioning deficits. Hypersensitivity. These are typical of a brain in development. But there is great evidence that mindfulness and related practices have positive effects on the brain regions that are most important to emotional balance, calm, and resilience, and all kinds of research showing the ways in which mindfulness helps kids with these issues.

You may be thinking to yourself, "That's all well and good, but how is my moody adolescent who can see only five seconds ahead going to sit down on a cushion and meditate?" The answer is, they don't have to. The next chapters will give you dozens of practices that are just as helpful as formal meditation and don't involve sitting still or take much time.

It's important to know that whether or not our kids practice, if we adults do everyone benefits from the infectious calm, clarity, and compassion fostered by mindfulness. When we can stay balanced with our own practice as our kids enter challenging years—whether it's the terrible twos or the terrifying teens—those phases go more smoothly for everyone.

BRAIN SCIENCE — IT'S NOT JUST FOR ADULTS

Understanding their own brains is empowering and motivating for kids. A study at Stanford examined how students' understanding of intelligence changed their work habits.[3] Two separate groups of middle schoolers were given a brief workshop in study skills, with a single difference: one group was taught about neuroplasticity and told that they could change their brains and become smarter by working hard. The kids from that group were easy to spot months later: they had better study habits and grades.

Kevin, a young man I work with, was skeptical about why he needed to address his stress. He had aced all of his science Advanced Placement tests and wasn't about to do anything in therapy without grilling me on the scientific evidence. I explained the mindfulness research and sent him some articles. Now he actually likes to visualize his prefrontal lobes growing ever so slightly during his mindfulness practices.

I've explained to many kids who see themselves as impulsive or just "bad" that they simply need to give their brain some exercise. When they take that perspective, they are able to let go of some of their shame and self-blame and begin to feel better about themselves.

Slowing Down Our Minds

Stress, like death and taxes, is a certainty in life. But too often, our reactions to stress make everything—physical health, mental health, and thinking—worse. Besides reshaping our brains and helping us cultivate better responses to stress, mindfulness practices provide counterbalances to our busy world, because they encourage us to slow down, stop the rush, *be* instead of *do,* and experience instead of think. These slow moments are often the moments when we feel and are at our best. Slowing down and being a little vulnerable is not easy, and for many kids, it may not feel safe. The world can be a scary place, but we can help them find those moments when they can be more mindful.

Consider where you do your best thinking or come up with your best ideas. Many people say, "In the shower." Why? Because we are relaxed, warm, comfortable, and often not in a rush. There are strong sensory stimuli—sounds, smells, sensations—that ground us in the present. Or perhaps you, like other great thinkers throughout history, receive insights as you daydream or drift off to sleep. Psychologists call this cognitive process *incubation,* and have discovered that flash insights are most likely to burst from the unconscious into the conscious mind at these relaxed moments, not when we are actively trying to make them happen.

Research shows that when the brain is relaxed, it takes in the big picture and opens to new ideas, making important new connections. The bumper sticker saying "Minds are like parachutes, they function best when open" does not just apply to politics; it holds true in learning, relationships, and creative approaches to life challenges.

Mindfulness practices open the mind in just this way. Think back to the exercise of making a fist: how clear were your thoughts compared to when you held your hands open in front of you?

For kids, the brain relaxes not only during mindfulness practices but also in free play, recess, vacations, nap time, daydreaming, doodling, and other nonacademic activities, all of which are falling by the wayside in our test-driven schools and achievement-driven culture. Young people from all walks of life are falling into the busyness trap. They are frequently overbooked and distracted, unfamiliar and uncomfortable with slowing down. We are speeding up our kids all the time, neglecting downtime or playtime in favor of more doing. The romantic notion of childhood as a time of wonder and freedom is slipping away.

While "doing" is important, it also exacerbates stress. The habit of staying busy gets hardwired into our brains at a young age, making it even more vital that kids learn how to slow down, as well as manage their responses to stress, before they become adults. There are many theories about why there has been such an explosion of mental illness in young people. I don't know the answer, or if there is even one—but this culture of doing and distraction certainly makes it worse.

The culture of "doing" has become ubiquitous. We can see it in all corners of our society, from the inner city, where kids are raised by video games inside or gangs in the streets outside, to the suburbs, where the culture of helicopter parenting emphasizes the college rat race, and kids are shuttled from soccer to SAT prep to saxophone lessons, all before homework. Everywhere, play, authentic connection, and curiosity are passively, if not actively, discouraged. I've encountered parents who have their sixteen-year-olds' "free time" scheduled into fifteen-minute increments and ask me when to fit in mindfulness practice. (I tell them, don't.) I've met college students whose parents track their phones by GPS to check on where they are at 3 a.m. A teacher at a workshop recently told me his school was cutting its lunch period from twenty to eighteen minutes. These are the extremes, to be sure, and yes, they may come from a place of concern, but they prevent children from learning from their own experiences. Kids are up to midnight or well past midnight online or studying, with no time to become curious about what matters to them.

Today's young people have less experience with slowing down and exploring the world around them, let alone exploring the beautiful worlds inside themselves. Many young adults with anxiety and depression say that the hardest times of day are when they have time to themselves. Yet getting curious about what's inside us is how our natural values arise, how true learning and growth takes place. When the cultural messages tell kids to ignore their experience, or that how they feel or look or what they do is wrong, they are left lacking in emotional intelligence and unprepared for adulthood. MIT sociologist Sherry Turkle reminded us in a 2012 TED talk, "If we don't teach our children to be alone, they're only going to know how to be lonely."[4]

I titled my first book *Child's Mind* to play on the Zen notion of beginner's mind. Zen master Shunryu Suzuki describes it this way: "In the beginner's mind there are many possibilities, but in the expert's mind, there are few."[5] The title *Child's Mind* was a call for adults and young people to return to the naturally contemplative state of childhood existence, that moment-to-moment open awareness with nonjudgment and acceptance and reflection. Contemplation, curiosity, wonder—these are the values of the beginner's mind. As we'll explore in chapter 2, experiencing things in their essence, for the first time, without judgment, is what mindfulness is about.

CHAPTER 2

mindfulness
what exactly is it?

> [T]he faculty of voluntarily bringing back a wandering
> attention, over and over again, is the very root of judgment,
> character, and will. No one is *compos sui* [master of oneself]
> if he have it not. An education which should improve this
> faculty would be *the* education *par excellence.*
>
> WILLIAM JAMES, *The Principles of Psychology*

Mindfulness seems to be everywhere these days. You may have heard about it from your company's human resources department, from your doctor or therapist, or even at your child's school. We see it on magazines in the checkout aisle of the grocery store and hear science stories about it on the radio. Dozens of mental health treatments incorporate mindfulness, and there are hundreds, if not thousands, of schools around the world bringing mindfulness to kids in their classrooms. But what exactly is mindfulness? I'll offer a definition below, but remember that for many kids (and adults), pictures, metaphors, stories, or experiences such as the exercise in chapter 1 that demonstrates the different stress responses using hand position and posture, may be more helpful than words.

While there are many ways to define mindfulness, they all share common elements. I like the definition "paying attention to the present moment with acceptance and nonjudgment." This definition has three critical elements:

1. paying attention on purpose
2. present moment contact
3. acceptance and nonjudgment

These three elements are the building blocks of mindfulness, the way arithmetic and algebra are the building blocks of calculus. This book includes practices that emphasize each element. Let's examine each in more detail.

Paying Attention

The idea of paying attention is often loaded. Think about the last time someone told you, "Pay attention." Did they say it to you in a kind and compassionate way? Did they teach you *how* to pay attention?

Now think about the last time you told a child in your life to pay attention, and consider the same questions. How disempowering must it feel, whether you struggle with attention or mental health issues or not, to be told to do something you have never been taught how to do. We ask our children to pay attention on a regular basis, but never teach them *how*. Mindfulness actually teaches kids how to pay attention and strengthens their attention, just as we teach kids to use and strengthen their muscles.

If the phrase "paying attention" still feels too loaded, you can offer words like *noticing* or *bringing awareness* in your definition.

Present Moment Contact

Many people, kids included, express skepticism at the value of this element of mindfulness. What is so great about the present moment, anyway? Well, when we are in the present, we are not in the future, worrying about some nightmare scenario that hasn't happened yet.

Nor are we in the past, reliving frightening or maybe just embarrassing experiences. I encourage kids to see the present moment as an *opportunity* for a rest, rather than a chore, so that they can let go of the past, whether that past involves something truly awful or just something dumb they said in the cafeteria. As we live in and open to the experience of the present moment, rather than the future or the past, we discover that the present moment is okay, maybe even interesting. Lao-Tzu, the father of Taoism, is said to have described depression as being stuck in the past and anxiety as being caught in the future—a description that makes intuitive sense to many of us.

Usually the present moment is not too bad. As human beings, we can tolerate just about anything for a moment, and, as I occasionally joke, the present moment does not last very long. The other good news is that being present makes us happy. A recent study discovered that *what* participants were doing was about half as important to their happiness as how focused they were on what they were doing in the present moment.[1] The same study found that our minds are wandering just about half the time, on average. And where do our minds wander? Usually to the past or the future.

My friend Mitch Abblett, PhD, a clinical psychologist and writer, suggests using the metaphor of the timeless machine, as opposed to the time machine. A time machine carries you to the past or future; a timeless machine keeps you fully in the present. What does the world look like from inside your timeless machine?

Acceptance and Nonjudgment

Being with and accepting what is happening in the present moment means not turning away or resisting, but it doesn't mean having to like what is happening. Rather, when we accept what is happening and give up the fight against it, we can find greater peace and perspective.

This element of mindfulness has been emphasized in recent years and in Western culture. I'm no anthropologist, but my guess is that the reason has something to do with our competitive individualistic society, which asks us to compare ourselves to others all the time.

In acceptance, we are *being* rather than just *doing*. That's not to suggest that doing is not important; it is, especially doing things in order to survive and create great civilizations. But getting off of autopilot and becoming aware of what we are doing is also important. Mind*less* doing has created much human suffering, at small and large scales. When we act mind*fully*, a better outcome is likely to arise.

With acceptance and self-acceptance, we learn to quiet the inner voice that judges us. This critical voice might be the echo of a caregiver, a snippy teacher, or even the voice of the larger culture that tells us we are inadequate or wrong because of our gender, sexuality, fashion sense, musical taste, or other identity markers. When we build self-compassion by accepting that thoughts, emotions, and bodies are what they are, we develop compassion for ourselves and others. As psychologist Carl Rogers put it, "[T]he curious paradox is that when I accept myself just as I am, then I change."[2]

My friend Fiona Jensen, a mindfulness educator, suggests that with younger children we say "kindness and curiosity" rather than "acceptance and nonjudgment."

Choosing What to Do Next

Mindfulness teacher Amy Saltzman adds another phrase to the end of the definition of mindfulness: *so we can choose what to do next.* Choice and freedom are what kids—what all of us—want. When we explain to kids that mindfulness is about their own choice and freedom, we pique their interest. Teens, especially, find themselves, and more freedom, among the most interesting subjects of all. An educator I met recently speaks of mindfulness as teaching "response-ability," or the ability to respond rather than react to challenging situations.

How We Develop Mindfulness: Practice and Practices

When people hear the word *mindfulness,* they often think of Eastern meditation—sitting cross-legged, back straight, very still, for long periods of time, with maybe some *om*-ing in there. But just as there are many different types of physical exercise, there are many different types of mindfulness practice. These include everything from guided visualizations to body-based relaxations to practices that boost concentration and compassion. We can think of them all as contemplative practices. All cultivate the three elements of mindfulness: paying attention, being in the present moment, and acceptance and nonjudgment.

To show you how mindfulness practices work, I will first explain the difference between mindfulness and concentration as forms of awareness. Most of us know what *concentration* means: a focused, single-pointed awareness—a zoom lens, a spotlight, a narrowing of attention onto something. Mindful awareness, or mindfulness, is the opposite; it is a wide-angle lens, a floodlight, an open and all-encompassing awareness. Both types of awareness are useful in our daily lives. Concentration, or focused awareness, is helpful when shooting an arrow, swinging a golf club, or doing homework; mindfulness, or open awareness, is important when driving, playing soccer, or brainstorming.

All practices that strengthen concentration or mindfulness use an anchor. They suggest resting our attention *on something*—the body, the breath, movement, the senses, an image, numbers, a word or phrase—to anchor ourselves to the present moment. While our thoughts might dwell on the past or race into the future, our bodies and five senses are always in the present and thus make good anchors. At teen mindfulness retreats, the typical recommendation is to make the anchor the breath, body sensations, or sounds. The anchor can also be movements, as movement in yoga, tai chi, and qigong. It can be music, chanting, or chimes; short phrases or prayers; or a visual image.

No matter what the anchor is, it is the nature of mind to wander away from it. Try resting your mind on something, and you'll soon find it wandering in the past, future, or elsewhere altogether. In a concentration practice, the goal is to notice this wandering and bring it back to the anchor, over and over again. This builds the strength of our concentration, as lifting a weight over and over again builds the strength of a muscle. The internal process might sound something like this: "Breathing . . . breathing . . . Mind is wandering. Okay, back to breath . . . Breathing . . . breathing . . ."

With a mindfulness practice, the goal is notice not only *when* the mind wanders, but also *where* the mind goes, before bringing it back to the anchor. The process sounds like this: "Breathing . . . breathing . . . Mind is wandering to worries about family . . . Gently bring it back to breath . . . Breathing . . . breathing . . ."

Mindfulness practices can be summed up with four Rs, which I learned from Vancouver-based mindfulness instructors Brian Callahan and Margaret Jones Callahan:

Rest awareness (the mind) on an anchor.

Recognize when and where it wanders.

Return awareness gently to the anchor.

And **repeat.**

Another way to understand the difference between mindfulness and concentration practices is to picture the mind as a puppy.

Concentration practice: Inevitably, the puppy wanders off. We bring it back as often as we need to.

Mindfulness practice: Inevitably, the puppy wanders off. We notice where it has gone and then gently, affectionately, we bring it back.

A BASIC MINDFULNESS MEDITATION PRACTICE

Take a moment right now to try a basic mindfulness meditation for yourself. Before you begin, adopt a posture that is both comfortable and sustainable for a few minutes, and then set a timer for three minutes.

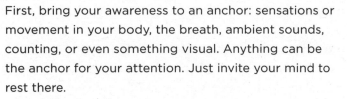 First, bring your awareness to an anchor: sensations or movement in your body, the breath, ambient sounds, counting, or even something visual. Anything can be the anchor for your attention. Just invite your mind to rest there.

Pretty soon, you will notice your mind begin to wander. *That is completely normal.* Each time you notice it wandering, notice where it goes and then gently guide your awareness back to your anchor.

Pretty simple, right? So simple, in fact, that it might seem like you're not doing very much. But don't be fooled. Every aspect of this practice is building the muscles of your mind.

- Each time you focus on or return to the anchor, you are building your concentration capacity.

- Each time you focus on the anchor, you detach from your thought stream. This is a practice of letting go in the moment, which translates to letting go in the rest of the world.

- Each time you notice that the mind is wandering, that is the moment of mindfulness—not a moment of failure.

- Each time you notice *where* the mind is wandering, that is an opportunity for insight into your mind's habits and patterns—what we might call wisdom or self-understanding.

Each of the mental actions in this practice strengthens neural connections that, with practice, rewire your brain, over time making mindfulness and compassion the automatic response to stress. As the saying goes, "neurons that fire together, wire together," and in this case, these are the concentration neurons, the awareness neurons, and the compassion and self-compassion neurons. We could all probably use more of those in our brains.

Over time, through mindfulness practice, we can build a map of the mind, notice our habitual thought patterns, and develop patience and compassion for our minds. Sakyong Mipham, a well-known Tibetan meditation teacher, speaks of this as "turning the mind into an ally."

MENTAL FITNESS

Humans evolved to need both physical exercise and mental exercise. Physically our ancestors were kept in shape by traveling as nomads, chasing animals, and harvesting food. Likewise, as I recently heard mindfulness teacher Jan Chozen Bays point out, we kept in shape mentally with activities such as being aware of the night sky as we navigated or gazing at the flowing river while we fished. These days, we need to build time into our lives for both physical and mental exercise.

Being Gentle and Compassionate With Ourselves

There is no problem with your mind wandering; that's the human mind doing what it does 47 percent of the time. The most important moment in mindfulness practice is the moment *after* the distraction. What do you do with it? What attitude do you have toward your mind? What tone of voice do you use when guiding it back to the anchor? Can you make a note of what your mind has done? Can you let go of any judgment and begin anew?

When we begin to practice mindfulness, our minds are untrained, but that's no reason to judge them harshly. We can just smile and recognize them as untrained, not judge them as bad or lazy or weak. Many of us drawn to mindfulness tend to be hard on ourselves, which, in moments of stress, leads to being hard on others. So, in mindfulness practice, it is important to bring the wandering mind back to the anchor *gently and compassionately.*

Think back to a puppy as a metaphor for the mind. How do you train a puppy? With a gentle firmness. If we train a puppy with nothing but harsh punishment, we end up with a mean and anxious puppy. If we don't train a puppy at all, we have other problems. It makes a mess, chases its own tail, or barks at nothing. Perhaps it becomes lazy and spoiled, or aggressive for no reason, or chases down every distraction. Having a well-trained puppy is a lot more fun than having an untrained one, even though the training may be hard work. A well-trained mind makes life easier and happier. So let's treat our minds as we would the puppy, with patient, good-humored encouragement.

Being gentle and compassionate with our own minds builds a habit of self-compassion, so that when we make a mistake we are kind to ourselves, rather than beating ourselves up. In turn, compassion for ourselves builds compassion for others, and we are able to approach stresses and disappointments with an attitude of befriending, rather than attacking.

Formal and Informal Mindfulness Practice

Mindfulness practices can be divided into two basic types: formal and informal. Ronald Siegel, Susan Pollak, Thomas Pedulla, and other mindfulness teachers use the metaphor of physical exercise to explain the difference.

Formal practice means setting aside a time of the day or the week to practice mindfulness meditation specifically. It is the mental equivalent of regularly going to the gym, to a yoga class, or for a run. Some people do their meditation at home; others go to a meditation center. Formal practice can also include setting aside a day or more for mindfulness meditation, usually away from home and regular life. Going on a mindfulness meditation retreat is roughly analogous to taking a weeklong backpacking trip or competing in a triathlon.[3]

Informal practice means deliberately bringing the elements of mindfulness to whatever we are doing in our daily lives. It's the mental equivalent of choosing to take the stairs instead of the elevator, biking to work, or carrying extra groceries. In an informal practice, we essentially make life itself the anchor of our practice, and learn to live life according to the insights of our practice. This doesn't have to be complicated; we can just pause and ask ourselves every so often, "What am I doing right now, and how do I know that?"

The two types of practice complement each other, and your mind will be in the best shape if you do both. However, doing both may not be realistic for every busy adult or kid.

What Mindfulness Is Not

What mindfulness is *not* is just as important as what mindfulness is, as many people continue to have misconceptions about it. This is important for you, but also important when you speak with kids and other adults about mindfulness.

MISCONCEPTION 1
Mindfulness Means Doing Nothing

Mindfulness really *is* doing something, even if, in a sense, it's *doing* nothing. Researchers have put mindfulness meditators in MRI machines to map their brains, and compared them to brains engaged in other activities. A brain doing mindfulness meditation is different from a brain that's spacing out, sleeping, relaxing, thinking, or working.[4] They also found that different types of meditation activate different parts of the brain.

MISCONCEPTION 2
Mindfulness Is Spiritual or Religious

One of the bigger misconceptions about mindfulness practices is that they are inherently religious or spiritual. Contemplative practices exist across cultures and across history, and they need not be associated with any one religion or even with spirituality at all. They can be completely secular mind-training practices. Many meditators do not identify as religious; many identify as atheist, and others do identify as Christian, Jewish, Muslim, Hindu, or Buddhist.

Jon Kabat-Zinn, who has done more to bring mindfulness into the mainstream than almost anybody in the West, deliberately kept his mindfulness-based stress reduction (MBSR) curriculum secular. Today, at least in many parts of the world, the word *mindfulness* holds not much more spiritual association than the word *concentration.* The word *meditation,* however, can still attract raised eyebrows; depending on where you live and work, *mindfulness* may as well.

Many people associate mindfulness with Buddhism. The historical Buddha did not *invent* mindfulness; no one can invent a state of mind. Nor did he *discover* it—at least, he was not the first, as everyone has had moments of quiet contemplation and present moment contact. But he did describe mindfulness and a system for cultivating it. Likewise, Sir Isaac Newton did not discover or invent gravity, but he studied and described it in ways that hadn't been done before.

MISCONCEPTION 3
Mindfulness Is Mysterious, Exotic, or Mystical

Most meditation teachers I've studied with are quick to point out the ordinariness of meditation and mindful awareness. But because of the way mindfulness has been portrayed in popular culture, many people think it is mystical or mysterious. The associations, accurate or not, with mysticism can be a draw for some kids and teens and an easy source of mockery for others. With a little experience, they soon discover that mindfulness practices are not necessarily mystical or transcendent.

MISCONCEPTION 4
Mindfulness Is a Way to Get High

Many mindfulness practices can make us feel very good, even blissful, right away, and mindfulness meditation's past association with the counterculture leads some to associate it with feeling high. Unfortunately, any "highs" we experience are not only not the point, they rarely last. A long-term practice means highs *and* lows and fascinating internal journeys—sometimes scary ones, sometimes mind-numbingly dull ones. In that sense, contemplative practice is a lot like life.

MISCONCEPTION 5
Mindfulness Is a Distraction Technique or Way to Escape Reality

Anyone who begins practicing mindfulness soon discovers it is not a way to escape or distract themselves from reality. Quite the opposite: it means facing reality in all its pain, boredom, and excitement. It may distract our thoughts from the past or future, but to do so, it will bring them into what's actually happening in the here and now.

A friend of mine refers to mindfulness as "universal exposure therapy." Exposure therapy is the idea that to overcome phobias, we gradually expose ourselves to them. Mindfulness exposes us to all the internal and external events that we fear, push away, and avoid.

We find many strange and wonderful things when we look inward. Sometimes we also find some frightening material, reminding us why we avoided looking within in the first place. The unpredictability of what we'll find when we look inward is also why, when we're getting started, we need the guidance and support of more experienced teachers.

A Jewish proverb suggests we "ask not for a lighter load, but for bigger shoulders to carry it." The quote captures how mindfulness works—not through dulling our perception of reality the way certain distractions, behaviors or substances will, but by strengthening us and making us larger in relation to life's pains. This is a radically different approach from what we in our culture usually teach our children, which is to fight, distract, or avoid. If some people find meditation an escape from reality too often, they are probably doing it wrong.

MISCONCEPTION 6
Mindfulness Is Shutting Off Your Thoughts

The point of mindfulness practice is not to shut off our thoughts, but to become more aware of our thoughts and distance ourselves from them. Shutting off thoughts is mind*less*ness, not mind*ful*ness. This is important to remember, as many beginners give up when they discover they cannot shut off their thoughts. You cannot (and probably should not) shut off your thoughts, just like you cannot and should not stop your breathing.

A useful analogy I've heard is that the brain secretes thoughts like the pancreas secretes insulin. Thinking is the brain's job, and we can't control it. But we can study the brain, learn its patterns and habits, and adjust ourselves to respond to our thoughts in different ways. (In fact, if we *didn't* have a wandering mind, we wouldn't have the opportunity to study and learn from its patterns and habits.) Meditation is not about simply what is or isn't happening in our minds, bodies, thoughts, or experiences; it is about how we relate to what's happening. The goal is to change our relationship to our thoughts.

MISCONCEPTION 7
Mindfulness and Meditation Are Quick Fixes

Our culture wants quick fixes. Yes, these practices can feel good, especially at first, which reinforces the motivation to practice. Some positive changes, including shutting off the fight-or-flight response when it is neither needed nor wanted, *can* occur quickly. But for the most part, mindfulness practices are about creating a slow internal evolution, rather than a quick revolution. Like physical exercise, the more we practice mindfulness, the more we benefit.

MISCONCEPTION 8
Mindfulness Is (Just) Relaxation or a Trance State

As described earlier, meditation is often relaxing and can trigger the relaxation response, but it is far more than that. Nor is it a trance state or hypnosis, though some guided visualization–style mindfulness practices are close cousins to certain kinds of hypnotic states.

MISCONCEPTION 9
Mindfulness Practices Are Self-Indulgent

When someone suggests that mindfulness is self-indulgent, I respond with a simple question: Do you know what the three leading causes of death are for young people in America? Cancer doesn't make the list, nor does drug overdose. The three leading causes of death among young people aged fifteen to twenty-four, according to the Centers for Disease Control and Prevention, are, in order, accidents ("unintentional injury"), suicide, and homicide.[5] Knowing this, consider what it would look like if our society was a little more mindful, paying attention to the present moment with gentleness and nonjudgment, compassion and self-compassion. We would likely have far fewer people dying before their adulthood has even begun. Bringing mindfulness practices to kids and teens is a public health intervention. (It's worth noting that when mindfulness teacher Thich Nhat Hanh was recently honored with an award from Harvard, it was not from Harvard Divinity School, nor from the Graduate School of Education, nor even the medical school, but from the Harvard Chan School of Public Health.)

Our culture tends to confuse and conflate ideas of self-care and self-indulgence. What some might call self-care is often self-indulgence, and vice versa. Bringing mindfulness to a wide audience truly is a public health intervention, because when we learn to care for ourselves, we are able to care for others. The research also shows that people who practice mindfulness eat and exercise better, along with other healthier decisions. Building compassion and more skillfully caring for the world around us is hardly self-indulgent.

MISCONCEPTION 10
Mindfulness Makes Us Passive or Weak

Mindfulness won't turn anyone into a doormat, or make us indifferent to danger. In fact, the research shows that meditators still get stressed and have emotional reactions, but bounce back faster than non-meditators. To put it another way, the storms still rise, but we can sail our ship through them calmly. That is what we want to give our young people: the ability to read their own emotional forecast and respond, to handle the stormy emotional times that are the stuff of life, rather than turning back or remaining stuck. It starts by being in the present moment, seeing what is, rather than escaping from it or distorting it. In this way, mindfulness practice makes us stronger and more able to respond to life, rather than passive and apathetic. And the science backs this too; mindfulness helps people become more resilient to traumas and setbacks, both large and small.

The idea that mindfulness strengthens us is an empowering one that resonates with today's kids. What I hear over and over again from young people who practice mindfulness is that they feel empowered, often for the first time, in their bodies, minds, and lives. This is because mindfulness is theirs; it is something no parent, no teacher, no bully, and no prison can take away. It is not a pill that a doctor tells them to take or a problem that a parent, teacher, or cop tells them to fix. No one even has to know they are practicing. Most of the exercises in this book are subtle enough to do silently in a chaotic classroom, in the outfield of a softball diamond, or backstage at the school play. Anyone can practice mindful movement in their room, while waiting in line, or even in a juvenile hall. Kids, and teens in particular, crave authenticity, ownership, and empowerment; mindfulness practice offers all three. Offering children the tools to find answers within, rather than by looking outside, is offering them the lifelong gift of independence.

CHAPTER 3

building the foundation
your own mindfulness practice

A woman sat outside a holy shrine, watching all the men
and women walk past the beggars, the sick, the elderly, and
the outcast, offering them nothing, hardly even seeing them.
Turning toward the sky, the woman cried out, "How can a
loving creator see the suffering I see and more, and do nothing
to help?" There was silence for a moment, and then a voice
responded. "I did do something, my child. I created you!"

A Sufi tale

⋃

One of the most common questions I hear from parents and professionals alike is, "What is the best practice for a kid who is in the
middle of a meltdown?" There is no magical breathing trick I can offer,
no mindful off-switch for a tantrum. The best practice for a kid in
meltdown mode is *your* practice. The nonreactive presence of an adult
and the wisdom and compassion we've gleaned from our own formal
and informal mindfulness practices—these are what a struggling kid
needs most. This chapter will explore how to establish and maintain
your own mindfulness practice—the most important and powerful
way you can share mindfulness.

The Research

Mindfulness and compassion start with us, and all the evidence suggests that, unlike outdated economic theories, mindfulness and compassion really do trickle down from us to the young people in our lives. This happens through modeling, which allows kids to see mindfulness, compassion, and their effects in action, and through mirror neurons, the parts of our brain that enable our kids to pick up on our emotions. (See "Facing Emotional Contagions" later in this chapter for more about mirror neurons.) We also demonstrate hard work and humility as we learn for ourselves the challenges and benefits of a regular mindfulness practice. What we learn from our own practice is directly applicable to the most difficult situations that we face as caregivers, including our kids' stubborn resistance or major meltdowns.

The research is clear: if you are a parent and practice mindfulness, you are likely to have a happier, healthier family with better communication and less conflict.[1] If you are a teacher and take care of your stress, the kids in your classroom will learn better and behave better.[2] If you are a doctor and work on your compassion, mindfulness, and people skills, your patients will trust your decisions, follow your advice, and heal faster. If you are a therapist, your attention and attunement to clients will increase, and your clients will improve faster—results that have been proven in placebo studies.[3]

Research has shown that mindfulness practice decreases burnout and compassion fatigue and increases empathy and effective communication. The best way to create stressed-out, unhappy kids is to surround them with stressed-out, unhappy adults. The opposite is also true: calm, compassionate adults are far more likely to lead to calm, compassionate kids and the conditions under which they can thrive. The best predictor of kids' stress levels is the stress levels of the important adults in their lives. After our son was born, our pediatrician told us, "I've seen a lot of anxious kids who don't have anxious parents, but I've almost never seen anxious parents who don't have anxious kids."

Starting and Maintaining a Mindfulness Meditation Practice

Many wonderful teachers have shared straightforward, universal advice on starting a mindfulness meditation practice. I strongly recommend that you find your own teacher or meditation center, if you can, to help you get started with your practice. Allow me also to give you some practical tips from my own experience as a meditator and meditation teacher.

The first question to ask is: When during the day do you have a few minutes you can set aside, even just five or ten? Early in the morning, at lunchtime, during your child's nap, or in the evening before bed? Since consistency is key to building a habit, it helps to find the same few minutes each day. If you can't identify any spare moments for meditation, don't worry. There are plenty of ways to incorporate mindfulness into your life by bringing more awareness to what you are already doing. (See chapter 11 for more on working with these little moments.)

Do you have existing habits you can build on already? When I was a teacher, I would get home from work, go jogging for half an hour, and immediately sit down to meditate after that. The habit of physical exercise was a simple foundation for mental exercise and also gave me a cognitive boost that helped me sit in focused quiet. Are there daily routines that practice can be linked into for you? Just as some fitness trainers advise you to just put on your running shoes, walk outside, and see what happens, many meditation teachers suggest, "Just sit on your cushion for a moment and see if you start practicing."

If you have a busy schedule, write your meditation time into your day planner or set a reminder on your phone. It may sound like overkill, but how many of us say, "If it's not in my planner, it doesn't exist"?

Like physical exercise, practicing mindfulness can be easier when done with friends or in a community. Are there friends or colleagues with whom you can sit and meditate on a somewhat regular basis? Is there a regular mindfulness group in your community? Your family may be a great reminder too, and you can inspire one another. Other people can be also helpful in giving you someone to talk to about your practice. Sharing the benefits and challenges of your practice can be inspiring. Do you have even one friend you can connect with regularly—by phone, email, text, or social media—to inspire each other? Research shows that when we tell other people we are going to do something, we are more likely to follow through. If you don't have someone to talk to about your practice, consider writing about your experiences in a journal.

Having a guided meditation CD, audio file, or app can help in the initial stages of establishing or reestablishing a formal practice. A regular, comfortable place to meditate is also helpful. Buying fancy equipment is not usually helpful or necessary, but just as the right shoes can make a difference to your physical workout, investing in a good meditation cushion, pillow, or bench, as well as finding a physical posture that suits you, will allow you to meditate in greater comfort.

Finding a posture that is upright, comfortable, sustainable, and that keeps you awake is the most important. Tap into your imagination. Some people find it helpful to imagine a string coming out of the top of their head and lifting them up; Jon Kabat-Zinn suggests sitting "nobly," like a king or queen on a throne. Legs can be folded or not, but making a tripod with your buttocks and feet is most stable. Your hands can rest in your lap or at your sides. Sitting is only one choice of posture; you can stand or lie down, provided the posture is comfortable and sustainable.

Lastly, set reasonable goals for your meditation practice—and maybe no goals around the outcome. If you decide to practice for an hour every day starting tomorrow, you are less likely to be meditating regularly in a year than if you start with five minutes on weekdays and ten on weekends, and build up from there. When you don't meditate, don't be too hard on yourself. Just as you redirect the mind during a mindfulness meditation, gently and compassionately bring yourself back to your meditation practice when you miss a regular session.

Meditation retreats are helpful, because they give you not only a place to meditate undisturbed, but, like training for a road race, also something to get in shape for. Going on a retreat also rejuvenates your home meditation practice. Consider finding a retreat, ideally one with people in your geographic or professional community with whom you can stay connected afterward.

When we have kids in our lives and homes, distractions are inevitable, and quiet, undisturbed moments become a scarce commodity. Having a regular, predictable meditation time will help them and you. Communicate to your family and children the importance of their support for your practice time. It helps you feel happier, calmer, and more patient. It quiets your loud mind or settles your thoughts—whatever the reason is for you. I always appreciate the writer Anne Lamott's line, "Almost everything will work again if you unplug it for a few minutes, including you." Asking them to support you may make them curious enough to join you.

The Power of Informal Mindfulness Practices

Can you find a moment to breathe? Is there time in your child's busy schedule or between your appointments when you can check in with yourself or eat your lunch mindfully? Are you singletasking and aware of what you are doing as you go through your day? Or are you operating on autopilot? Many informal practices remind us of the power (and challenge) of doing one thing at a time, quiet our own self-defeating criticism with self-compassion, reconnect us with the mindfulness we already have, and cultivate wisdom and perspective to keep moving forward in this journey.

SINGLETASKING

A simple way to bring mindfulness into our everyday lives is to let go of our multitasking habits and embrace singletasking. All of us try to multitask, but it can really stress us out. Research shows that multitasking is a myth. What we think of as multitasking is, in fact, paying attention to one thing after another in very rapid succession, and studies show that we end up getting half as much done in twice the time. However, because busyness is stimulating and feels good (and we actually do get a dopamine rush from being busy), multitasking reinforces the illusion of being efficient, making it a hard habit to break.

My friend Peter, himself a therapist and mindfulness practitioner, was in the midst of a crazy day, cooking dinner, fielding a work emergency, and dealing with the stress and logistics of trying to buy a house while his wife was out of town. When his eight-year-old son asked him for help with his homework, Peter snapped.

"I can't do six different things at once," he barked. "I can only do one thing at a time!"

His son was first taken aback, then looked up at him curiously and asked, as only a child can, "Well, Dad, then why don't you?"

Singletasking, doing just one thing at one time, is important to staying balanced. The following simple practice demonstrates the power of singletasking—of slowing down and paying attention to just one thing in the present moment.

> With your eyes open or closed, place one finger gently in the center of your forehead.
>
> Just feel your finger against your forehead.
>
> And feel the sensations of your forehead against your finger.
>
> You might notice temperature, texture, moisture, even detect your pulse.
>
> Stay with this awareness a moment longer. If the mind wanders, just gently bring it back to the sensation of your finger on your forehead.
>
> Then open your eyes, take your hand down, and notice how you feel.

If you noticed your experience, then you have experienced mindfulness.

GIVING YOURSELF A BREAK

Many of us feel under tremendous pressure to be the perfect parent, the most inspirational teacher, or the most charismatic helper who can save all the suffering children. Many of us have a critical inner voice telling us we aren't doing enough. The internal critic may echo voices from our childhood or the voices of oppression and bigotry in our society.

There are also very real external pressures—the judgments of other parents, high-stakes academic testing, schools or organizations that value numbers over nuance. Feelings of inadequacy and worry are passed on to us unconsciously, and we unconsciously pass them on to our children. Most of us have a basic human desire to be liked, and we all want to be seen as competent by others, but such constant comparisons create still more anxiety. Whatever its source, our internal critic is difficult to ignore, and it manifests in subtle and insidious ways in our lives, compounding the ten thousand joys, sorrows, and stresses that come from spending time with young people.

Parents are under incredible pressure, and even in the "caring professions" there is an incredibly high rate of burnout, substance abuse, turnover, and compassion fatigue. This is what makes mindfulness, compassion, and self-compassion some of the most important practices we can do for ourselves and model for the people around us. They are true self-care. Bringing mindfulness to certain activities—mindfully eating chocolate, for example—can feel like both self-care and self-indulgence.

CONNECT TO SEEDS THAT ARE ALREADY PLANTED IN YOU

I did not learn to meditate when I was a child. My parents were not particularly religious, though they were certainly spiritual; they did not formally teach me mindfulness. Yet when I became interested in mindfulness as a young adult and reflected back on my life, some of my most cherished childhood memories were brimming with both mindfulness and compassion. Watching clouds form and unform in the summer sky with my father, walking with silence and purpose as I listened to the sounds of the forest at nature camp, focusing my breath to create the biggest and roundest soap bubble I could before it popped—these moments included many of the elements of mindfulness.

Take a moment to think back to your own childhood. Are there any memories from childhood or other times in life that capture elements of mindfulness—paying attention to the present moment with acceptance and nonjudgment?

When I ask people from around the world this question, some common themes emerge. Most often, the sounds, scents, tastes, or other sensations are a part of the memory. Our senses are always in the present, even when our minds are racing to the past or future. Often, the memorable mindful scenes take place in or close to nature, with feelings of warmth and safety.

You needn't even go back to childhood; just consider the everyday moments in which you may experience mindfulness today, or how you could bring mindfulness to gardening, walking, preparing dinner, or other daily activities.

If you are new to mindfulness, consider what familiar experiences may have already allowed you to experience the elements of mindfulness. Perhaps you have practiced yoga or tai chi, enjoyed a guided visualization, or tried progressive muscle relaxation or hypnosis—all close cousins of mindfulness. It is likely that mindfulness has more in common with your values, interests, and activities than you might have initially thought.

FACING EMOTIONAL CONTAGIONS

In spending time with kids, we inevitably come into conflict when our own wishes and needs conflict with theirs. When we find ourselves entrenched with an angry or emotional child, it is hard not to become angry ourselves. Emotions, particularly strong emotions in people we care about, are contagious. But just as so-called negative emotions are contagious, so are calming and compassionate ones.

As described in chapter 1, mirror neurons in the brain are what cause us to feel the experiences and emotions of people around us. In the classic example, if I am watching you eat a banana, the neurons in my brain that are involved in eating bananas begin to fire. Likewise, if I am sitting across from you and feeling sad or angry, you are likely to have those neurons fire in your brain as well; thus you are *feeling* those emotions yourself, not just detecting them.

We are constantly absorbing emotions from those around us. That's part of the reason being around kids and teens, with their roller coasters of emotion, can be so exhausting. When our own hearts and minds are clouded by emotion, we are not showing up and responding with our wisest mind and most open heart. Our capacity for calm in the midst of a kid's emotional storm offers hope, because it signals that calm is possible in the midst of chaos.

Conflict, with our kids and with one another, is inevitable. While we may try to avoid it, research shows that for kids, seeing conflict is not necessarily problematic. What is most important is how we act—what behaviors we model—when we are in conflict and in resolution. This also means that it's up to us, as adults, to take the lead and demonstrate that it is possible to calm down and reconnect—with our kids, with others involved in the conflict, and with ourselves.

What are some techniques you have used to help your children stay calm? What was your emotional state at those times? What about times when they, or you, became more upset? What was your emotional state at those times? These questions help you build on your own experience.

Of course, maintaining our cool in the midst of a child's cries or teenager's tantrum is far easier said than done. There are a few approaches we can take. Telling an angry child to practice mindfulness to calm down is far less likely to succeed than calming *ourselves* down. The best way to do this is to have a solid foundation in formal and informal mindfulness practice, which rewires our brain to attend and befriend our unhappy child, rather than fight or avoid them. Remember, when we are angry, we see only threats, and not the big picture.

In those moments, it can be hard to remember the breath. Other informal mindfulness practices can help. We can change our minds by changing our bodies. Try bringing your awareness into your feet, unclenching your fists, sitting down or leaning back, and feel the sensations. You can also look around the entire room or glance out the window for a moment to gain perspective, before reengaging.

Still, if we lose it, sometimes we lose it. The best thing to do when this happens is to forgive ourselves (employing self-compassion), reflect on what happened, and talk about our behavior with our kids as soon as we can once we are calm. Taking responsibility for our words and actions is the best way to teach them to take responsibility for theirs.

HOW DO I KNOW?

To paraphrase my friend and fellow therapist Ron Siegel, things generally work best when everyone is *present* in the room.

One of the simplest practices for staying present and anchored to your present moment experience is to ask yourself throughout your day, "How do I know I'm doing what I'm doing?" Check in with all of your senses, including your thoughts and feelings. How do I know I am listening to my kids? Am I waiting and thinking of a response before they even finish speaking, or am I open to their ideas? How do I know I am teaching? I hear my voice speaking and see that the kids are tuned in—at least somewhat. How do I know I am driving? I can feel the car vibrating, the engine roaring, and see the landscape moving past.

WHAT WENT WELL?

Mindfulness teacher Sharon Salzberg reminds us that to do anything challenging long-term, be it parenting, teaching, or the work of healing, we make a deliberate practice of seeing and connecting with the positive resilience and humanity in others and ourselves. With that in mind, take a moment to connect to the positive. Which children or adults in your life inspired you today with their creativity or resilience? Which of your colleagues or mentors? What and who has sustained you in challenging times in the past? What successes have you had today, this week, or this year that you can hold on to? Quaker educator and author Irene McHenry suggests asking yourself, "What went well?" on a regular basis. You can also ask, "What's *not* wrong?" It's a good practice to do for ourselves, but also with our partners or coworkers when we sit down to review the day together or in a meeting. Likewise, don't forget to offer your gratitude and appreciation to your kids, partner, and coworkers, in person or electronically.

When you connect with the positive, take time to really feel those experiences and allow them to sink in. Research shows that negative perceptions are encoded and stored instantly in the brain, going into the evidence files in our mind that tell us the world is a negative place. Positive perceptions take longer to encode—twenty to thirty seconds. So take a moment now, about thirty seconds, to contemplate and savor the positive in your day so far—feel those emotions, and allow them to penetrate to your core and reshape your outlook.

Consider also writing down what has gone well to have something to look back on, and consider sharing this appreciation practice with your kids on a regular basis.

GOING WITH YOUR GUT

One of the challenges of working with children is that we often get stuck and have to make a hard decision, but don't know what to do. Kelly McGonigal is a Stanford psychologist who teaches body awareness through practices like yoga. She suggests a simple practice for making a challenging decision, which I have adapted here. Some people call this practice "listening to your belly brain."

Take a moment, find a comfortable posture, and close or rest your eyes where they won't be distracted.

Bring the important decision to mind. Ask yourself, "What do I truly want in this situation?"

Imagine that you've made the decision in one direction. Tell yourself, "I have decided to do _____. I'm going to do it. My mind is made up." Make this decision as vividly as possible in your imagination.

As you do, quickly scan your body, noticing how it feels. Notice the quality of your breath and any tension. Bring special awareness to sensations in your torso and what messages they might be sending you. Note these quietly to yourself.

Take a breath, and release that decision scenario from your mind. Take a few deep breaths, allowing your body and mind to reset.

Now, reverse the scenario. Tell yourself, "No, I'm not going to do that. Instead, I've made up my mind to _____. That's what I'm definitely going with." Once more, make this scene as vivid as possible in your imagination.

Scan your body. Observe your breath. Notice sensations throughout your torso, particularly in your heart and gut, and what your body is communicating to you. Note these quietly to yourself, along with anything else that might arise.

I do this practice myself before making important decisions and share it often with my patients. A fifteen-year-old girl I saw recently spent most of our therapy session agonizing about whether to break up with her boyfriend. She sat on my couch, eyes closed yet attentive as I guided her through the practice. We finished, and her eyes snapped open. "I have to break up with Jamie!" she announced, without skipping a beat. Another student I see used this practice to make the tough choice between two top colleges she had been accepted to.

The Importance of Your Own Practice

In training to be a therapist, I was reminded that I have no scalpel or hammer; the tool I work with is myself. The same is true for parenting or any other ways we work with kids. If your body, mind, and heart are the tools, you need to train with them, maintain them, sharpen them, know their quirks, recognize that they will change over time, and realize what happens when they've been working overtime. Mindfulness practice is a way of doing that.

Self-care is critical in staying connected long-term and not getting burned out with compassion fatigue. How much time are you taking to care for yourself? Are you singletasking throughout your days? Are you taking moments to connect with your breath and touch the present moment? Are you being compassionate and generous to yourself as well as to others? Are you remembering where you drew strength from in other challenging times?

Writer, teacher, and activist Parker Palmer, in his inspiring book *The Courage to Teach,* reminds us that we "teach who we are." The principle applies to all of us. We give care from our best and worst selves, teaching and modeling for those who look up to us, whether we want them to in every moment or not. Many of us are in chaotic environments—our homes, hospitals, camps, or schools. Our work with kids is often undervalued, underpaid, and invisible. Without external or internal support, we can experience compassion fatigue and burnout, no matter how much we love our kids.

Learning to value ourselves and take time for self-care is important to our ability to be fully present for and connected with kids. We must learn to be present for ourselves before we can be present for anyone else. Then we can connect with kids from a place of grounded equilibrium, informed by insights from our own practice. I find that because of my mindfulness practice, I can tune in to the reality of a situation and listen to what is happening underneath the words of my clients and other people in my life.

When I was working in the inner city, I had a caseload of angry young men, one in particular whom I remember well, a Cape Verdean immigrant named Adriao, whose early adolescence was spent in and out of state care and state custody. I struggled to feel a connection with the twelve-year-old who, when he wasn't suspended or in custody, strutted around middle school, shoving classmates and swearing at teachers, but would sit in my office quietly and play with action figures. For a number of reasons, I left that job and had to break the news to the kids. I didn't think Adriao would care or even notice.

"Naw, you can't leave, Dr. Willard. You *can't* leave! I'm gonna go down to your new job and drag you back here to the therapy room, with your head banging on the stairs the whole way up. Then I'm gonna get my gun, and write Dr. Willard in bullet holes on the wall! No, you *can't* leave!" he protested.

Many people might have heard an angry young man—a threatening or dangerous young man. Maybe he was some of those things at certain points in his life, but what I heard underneath was, "I will miss you." I reflected that to him, in my language: "I'm gonna miss you too, Adriao."

Mindfulness allows us to discern what we are truly hearing or seeing, to look and listen deeply, and to hear the truth underneath the suffering of those around us and even our own suffering. When we can do that, kids will notice and open to our ideas.

Mindfulness practices help us to become comfortable with ourselves. When I was starting out in my therapy work, I had a wise old therapist, and I desperately wanted to be the wise old therapist. But that wasn't who I was. I'm also not the freestyle-rapping, basketball-playing therapist, like some of my coworkers are, and for a time I put myself down for that. At some point, I realized I have my own strengths as a middle-aged dorky therapist and should play to those. Now that I'm a parent, I know what some of my strengths are, and I know to ask for help with what I need to work on. Comfort with ourselves sends a strong message. No matter how nerdy or uncool we think we are, when we show kids that we are okay with ourselves, we tell them that it is okay to be themselves, whoever that might be. Messages of acceptance and self-acceptance, implicit or explicit, are of the utmost importance for young people. Mindfulness can be a big part of that.

Practicing mindfulness also helps us to be more authentic. Authenticity is something that young people crave. They have great bullshit detectors, which is why they can be intimidating. The desire for authenticity is partially hardwired into the adolescent brain. For many kids, being able to detect authentic intentions, hidden agendas, and true motivations is a matter of survival, especially if they've been through hard times. The more authentic we can be, the more authentic and trusting our relationship with kids will be.

When we know and accept ourselves, we will be at our best for our kids. We can know what our strengths are and work from them, rather than from our blind spots.

It's been said that mindfulness meditation strengthens two qualities: wisdom and compassion. Are there any two qualities more worth cultivating for our time with young people?

DRIVING YOURSELF MINDFUL

A meditation teacher once suggested that I drive one leg of my commute once a week without listening to the radio, talking on the phone, or drinking my coffee. I didn't think much of the idea at first, but when I tried it, I felt the vibrations of the car, the sounds of the engine that reminded me to shift gear. I was much more aware of the thoughts and feelings that arose as I cut even one or two distractions out of this regular activity. I don't drive my entire commute this way every day, but I do set aside distractions for the first and last few minutes of my drive, starting from the stoplight nearest my house. Bringing mindfulness to these parts of my drive helps ease my transition into the next space and allows me to be truly present when I arrive. Doing the same thing starting from the first or last stop on the subway or bus might work for you, if you don't commute by car.

PART II

practices for children and teens

CHAPTER 4

introducing mindfulness to kids

Prevent trouble before it arises.
Put things in order before they exist.

LAO-TZU, in *A Thousand Names for Joy*
by Byron Katie and Stephen Mitchell (translator)

∪

When we begin to share mindfulness with kids, the first big question is often, "How do I get them interested?" How can we make mindfulness fun and accessible to young kids and relevant for older kids? Even when they don't give us that skeptical look, kids come with a range of backgrounds, attention spans, learning styles, and interests.

Step 1: Take Time to Prepare the Soil

The first step in introducing mindfulness to kids is to ensure that you have a good relationship with them. That good relationship can emerge out of your own mindfulness and compassion practices, which help you to stay connected and compassionate with your kids. When kids trust and connect with you, in general and in the moment, they are more likely to give the whole mindfulness thing a try. If you meet with a lot of resistance, you may need to slow down and reinvest your time in the relationship in other ways. Your relationship with your child is more important than mindfulness, and mindfulness is unlikely to grow in a strained relationship. If your kids are resisting more than just mindfulness, and your relationship is strained, consider enlisting the help of another adult whom they look up to, such as a coach, teacher, or therapist.

Step 2: Assess What You Can— and Cannot—Change

The second step is setting and knowing your intentions, even if they are a little mixed. There is often an underlying agenda—usually behavior change that you (or a school or concerned professional) want to see. Yet offering mindfulness practices with the agenda of change can send kids the message that they are broken and in need of fixing—an unhelpful message, which they may also be getting elsewhere in their lives and which may put them on the defensive.

Instead of thinking about how you want the kids to change, consider the changes you can and want to make. You can't change the kids or expect them to adapt to your teaching style. All you can do is change how you relate to them, encourage change in their environment, or change the way you teach them. Ultimately, all you are ever really doing is creating the conditions under which change is most likely to occur.

Step 3: Consider Your Kids

The third step is to think about your kids' interests and personalities. What naturally draws their interest? A kid who loves sports might be motivated to learn mindfulness if she can do so by exploring movement or body-based exercises. A kid who loves art could be introduced to mindfulness through mindful drawing or sculpting, or observation activities. A nature lover might be drawn to mindfulness through the promise of experiencing a deep connection to the natural world.

If your child is interested in . . .	try these practices:
Sports	Breathing with All Our Senses • Child's Eyes • Zoom Lens and Wide Lens • Sensory Awareness Walking • Penny Walking • Tree Practice • What Went Well? • The Human Mirror • Human Kaleidoscope
Creative arts (e.g., drawing, design, photography, filmmaking)	Clearing the Clouds • Seeing with Different Eyes • Zoom Lens and Wide Lens • Sensory Awareness Walking • Shades of Green • The Color Detective
Nature, outdoor activities	Basic Walking Meditation • Sensory Awareness Walking • Appreciative Walking • Surfing the Soundscape • The Color Detective • Shades of Green • Artist's Eyes • Samurai's Eyes • Seeking Stillness • Clouds in the Sky • Zoom Lens and Wide Lens
Social media	Social Media Meditation • The Seventy-Ninth Organ • THINK Before You Speak
Being a good friend, making new friends	Going with Your Gut • Smile Meditation • Pass the Breath • The Human Mirror • Metta Breath • Butterfly Hug • Personal Space Practice • What Went Well? • THINK Before You Speak
Academics, general	STOP • 7–11 Breath • Sensory Breathing • 3-2-1 Contact • Just BE x 3 • Clearing the Clouds • The Stone in the Lake
Writing	Write Your Own Mindful Breathing Meditation • SIFTing Our Experience

Music	Find the Song • One-Track Mindfulness Practice • Surfing the Soundscape
Performing arts (e.g., acting/ drama, singing, instrumental performance, slam poetry)	7-11 Breath • STOP • Seeking Stillness • Metta Practice • Metta Breath

Another way to start is to try the practices in this book for yourself, explore what resonates for you and why, and then share these with your kids. You can explain to your kids that you like to clear your head after work by taking a few 7–11 breaths while you wait for your tea water to boil, or mindfully walk from your car to your office and notice one beautiful thing, or take the first bite of a meal mindfully, or listen to five sounds in the morning before you get out of bed.

If your child is struggling with a learning or psychological issue, ADHD, or depression, consult the appendix. It will help you find the practices in this book that match your child's needs. If your child is working with a therapist, you might ask the therapist if it makes sense to incorporate mindfulness into the therapy or into family life. The therapist may also have more success than you in getting your kids to try mindfulness practices!

Bullying is, thankfully, an issue that has been recently receiving the attention it deserves. Kids can practice guided visualizations, like the Tree Practice and the Stone in the Lake, to help themselves feel more confident in challenging situations. Other practices, such as the shorter breath practices in chapter 11, may help them stay calm even when they are feeling scared or overwhelmed.

Step 4: Bring It Up and Generate Buy-In

Tailoring your pitch to the individual kid is the key to making mindfulness appealing and inspiring them to try mindfulness practices, formal or informal. While only you know what will catch your kids' attention, here are some ideas to help you craft your approach.

Tap in to their desires. You can tell your kids you've heard that mindfulness helps with socializing, school, sports, performance—whatever may be motivating them in that moment. You can also discuss with them how much they may be missing out on by not paying attention to their internal experience and to the world around them. (Adolescents often talk about FOMO—fear of missing out.) YouTube videos that demonstrate this concept include those showing violin maestro Josh Bell playing in the subway or those showing the infamous "invisible gorilla" selective-attention test. We adults like to remind kids that they are missing out on life or material from class, but they may be more interested in hearing that they might be missing out on a smile from that cute boy, a fly ball in the outfield, or a potential friendship, if they aren't paying attention.

Identify role models. A colleague a few years back joked, "Thank God the Seahawks just won the Super Bowl. They meditate, and now I have something to share with the kids!" It's easy to do an online search for "[*blank*] who meditate," and fill in the blank with *musicians, actors, athletes, scientists, politicians* or maybe even *CEOs*—whoever your kid looks up to. We adults are never as sly as we think, but we can always drop into conversation that we heard that this pop star or that athlete practices mindfulness.

Pique their curiosity. My dad introduced me to mindfulness when I was about seven by saying, "Hey, want to see a magic trick?" He then showed me how to make clouds move and disappear with each breath.

Discuss stress and its effects. When I speak to kids professionally, I often start with the four-part exercise from chapter 1, which demonstrates how our bodies and minds work together to affect how we think and feel. High school kids immediately grasp how stress interferes with their academic and social lives.

Be aware that stress management as a motivator can cut both ways. Certainly adults worry about stress and kids complain about it, but it may also be a badge of honor. I led a mindfulness group at a high-powered school recently and advertised it with two sets of signs around campus: one advertising the mindfulness group, and the other advertising a stress-reduction group. I received almost ten times as many inquiries about the mindfulness group as I did about the stress-reduction group. That's why doing the four-part demonstration exercise is helpful: it shows the negative effects of stress.

Enlist the help of other kids. Testimonials from other, older kids can also be valuable. Parents might enlist the kids of family friends who practice mindfulness, especially those who are successful academically, athletically, or creatively. In a school, getting graduates of a mindfulness group to come back and say how mindfulness has affected their lives may be a lot more inspiring than anything you could say.

Emphasize freedom. Teens specifically appreciate the freedom that comes from mindfulness practice. They appreciate seeing that they actually have choices, have power in their lives, and that they can discover these through mindfulness. The message that mindfulness will not change the external circumstances of their lives but can change their internal reactions to it may be novel and appealing. Mindfulness doesn't get rid of anything, but it puts things in perspective and strengthens our ability to handle difficulties without being destroyed or controlled by them. Recently I heard someone say, "To feel better, we need to get better at feeling," which is exactly what mindfulness teaches. When kids can see clearly their own thoughts and feelings, negative behaviors are less likely.

My colleague Sam Himelstein asks kids in trouble with the law, "How much time did you spend thinking about what got you into prison, or into trouble? And how much time have you spent thinking about it since?" This is a particularly stark example of how pausing before acting can impact our freedom, but it holds true for any kid who's been in a time out, grounded, or in detention.

Ask them to help you with your practice. When we give kids special responsibility, they often rise to the occasion, finally feeling recognized for being older and more mature. Giving them the job of being your timer or bell ringer when you practice may inspire them to join you. You can ask them to lead you in some shorter guided meditation practices as they learn to read. If your kids are older, you and they can take turns reading guided meditations to each other. And asking them to remind you to breathe or do just one thing at a time when *you* look or act stressed out creates a lot more buy-in when it comes time to playfully remind them of the same.

Do informal practices with them. Practicing mindfulness together with your kids is ideal. Kids want quality time with us, and vice versa, so why not make it mindful? And remember, mindfulness practice doesn't have to be done on a meditation cushion. Taking a walk without your phone, preparing and eating a meal, listening to music, playing a game, and everything else you do already as a family can be done mindfully, if you are offering the activity and/or each other your full attention.

Many families say a prayer or a word of thanks around the family dinner table; you could make a small ritual of doing a short, informal mindfulness practice before meals. You might start with Soup Breathing (chapter 11), Surfing the Soundscape (chapter 8), or taking the first one or two bites of your meal mindfully (see chapter 6, Mindful Eating). Consider adding a practice to transition times, such as your pre-bedtime ritual, particularly for younger kids or those who struggle to fall asleep. Helpful practices for these times are the Stone in the Lake (chapter 5), Clearing the Clouds (chapter 9), What Went Well? (chapter 3), and the Metta (Lovingkindness) Breath (chapter 11). Chapter 11 offers more ideas for incorporating short, informal mindfulness practices into your everyday life.

Be honest and realistic. However you start the conversation, be straightforward and don't be an evangelist. Young people appreciate honesty from us. Rather than promising that mindfulness will be a cure-all, you could say, "This might help" or "Lots of kids like you have found this helpful and fun." Don't promise what mindfulness practice can't deliver. I've even said to kids, "This may sound kind of goofy, or feel a little awkward, but give this a try, and we can laugh about it afterward if it's too weird."

Working with Your Intentions and Expectations

One of the most challenging aspects of sharing mindfulness practices with kids is working with our own expectations. Wise words from a friend once taught me that "expectations are disappointments waiting to happen." This is because suffering arises when we are attached to a particular outcome but reality has a different idea. This can lead to burnout when things don't work out, or hubris when they do.

When it comes to sharing mindfulness with kids, having too strong an expectation or agenda is dangerous. If you are reading this book with the expectation that all the kids in your life will be happily meditating away and enjoying the fruits of mindfulness practice, you are apt to be disappointed, and I'll be checking my inbox for your angry emails. Instead of having high expectations or narrow agendas, I invite you to connect instead with your own intention in sharing, regardless of what outcome may arise. If your intention is for the benefits of mindfulness to somehow trickle down to the kids in your life and to learn a few practices you and they can do together, or they can sometimes do independently, you will find what you are looking for.

If you set intentions rather than goals or expectations, you focus on a process you *can* influence, rather than the outcome, which you cannot control. Intentions tell us where we are, keeping us focused on the journey rather than the destination. Make good plans, and even backup plans, but be willing to go in an unexpected direction if that's where the road takes you, and just appreciate and learn from what you find on your journey.

When we intend to offer kids the experience of mindfulness, rather than expecting them to jump into their own independent practice, we can all relax as we let go of attachments to outcomes and stay present with what is. And when our intention is just to share a positive experience of mindfulness, we all experience peace, whatever the outcome.

Perhaps the best intention we can have is to create a connection with the kids in our lives while teaching them some awareness. The more this can truly be our intention, the better for the kids, the relationship, and our own sanity. In the end, an authentic human connection will be more helpful to them than any specific mindfulness practice.

Connect with Your Own Intentions

Intention is like a highlighter pen for your mind. Contemplating intention keeps our priorities in sight as life rushes by.
ETHAN NICHTERN, author and Buddhist teacher

So much of our work with kids starts with the internal work of knowing ourselves and our own intentions. Reflect on what mindfulness means to you. *Why* do you want to share mindfulness with your kids? What do *you* want? What is your intention, and is that intention in keeping with the core elements of mindfulness practice? Plenty of parents come to me, a therapist who teaches mindfulness to kids, because they want their kid to gain an edge academically, on the soccer field, or with their violin solo, but these parents also move slowly and with integrity, honoring the original intentions of mindfulness practice.

To help you see and clarify your intentions, take five or ten minutes now for this reflection practice.

Begin by becoming present. As you make contact with the present, allow yourself to let go of the day behind you and ahead of you. Notice the residue that you carry and allow it to fall away. Set down any anxiety or stress, knowing you can always pick it up again after this practice.

Reflect for a moment about what you hope to get out of this book. Then reflect on what or who drew you to this notion of sharing mindfulness with young people.

Reflecting more deeply, consider what really brought you a wish to share mindfulness in this way.

Consider what brought you personally to mindfulness meditation or mindfulness practice. For many of us, it was suffering. Perhaps it was your own suffering, perhaps it was seeing suffering in the world, or perhaps it was seeing someone you love suffering deeply. Or perhaps it was a loss or near loss: death, sickness, old age, mental illness, addiction.

Now, recall the moment when a mindfulness practice really clicked for you.

Examine, too, your motivation for sharing mindfulness with the young people in your life. Perhaps it is your own suffering as a child or seeing another child suffer. Perhaps it is something else from your family or childhood experience. Perhaps it is a drive for justice, a personal or cultural value to be of service, a desire to heal the world, or a wish to share the joy in some way. From where and when did that calling arise?

Now, reflect on what you hope to learn from this book. As you do, reflect also on what you are hoping to offer others after reading this book.

Create Conditions for Mindfulness to Grow

One of my mentors, psychologist Ed Yeats, recently said of both therapy and parenting, "It can be frightening, because you have far less power than you think you should have, and yet so much more power and influence than you realize." Some kids will love the mindfulness practices you choose to share with them, and the seeds will blossom right away. Some kids may not appreciate the practices or your efforts, but that doesn't mean you've failed to plant seeds.

Years ago I worked with a man who had just finished a prison sentence for an armed robbery he had committed in the throes of addiction. He was excited about the mindfulness group I offered at the halfway house.

"I've been practicing yoga and meditation every day in prison for the last eight years!" he told me.

I was thrilled. "Wow, I didn't realize that they taught yoga in prison," I said.

"Oh, no," he swiftly corrected me. "A yoga teacher came in once, like, eight years ago and taught us a few poses and some breathing, and I've been doing it ever since." Without guidance, his yoga had probably evolved into some unconventional postures in the intervening time, but his commitment to practice and what he got from it never wavered. We don't know what seeds we may be growing, even as our kids protest loudly or silently roll their eyes at our attempts to teach mindfulness.

If, after sharing mindfulness practices from this book, the kids in your life are not meditating on their own, that does not mean you have failed. Even if the kids are screwing around when you are trying to share practices with them, you aren't necessarily wasting your time, and neither are they wasting yours. See what lessons you can draw. Countless kids who seemed to be not paying attention when I taught them mindfulness practices have come back to me months, or even years, later to tell me how helpful the practices were at a later point in their lives, when they needed them. I've also had parents tell me that their own practice was far more important for their family than anything they tried to teach their kids.

Parenting is about creating and seeing teachable moments —opportunities for kids to grow and gain insights. All teaching is about creating conditions for learning, and so our job is to find, create, and use those moments.

Actions Speak Louder Than Words

Preach the Gospel. If necessary, use words.

Attributed to ST. FRANCIS OF ASSISI

I've always taken this quote to mean that whatever our faith is, we should live it, and that our actions preach our faith more powerfully than our words do. I mentioned it earlier, but it bears repeating: the best way to share mindfulness with our kids is to practice mindfulness ourselves.

Sharing anything starts with having an abundance of it to share, and mindfulness practice is no different. It is shared best, and most authentically, when it emerges from our own practice. Not many of us would trust our child with a lifeguard whose only training came from *Baywatch*, or climb a mountain with a guide who has read *The Snows of Kilimanjaro* but never slept a night under the stars. When we are guiding others on an inner journey, we need to know something about where we're going and what we might encounter. When we have a mindfulness practice of our own, we can share and teach from our own experience. Our practice also keeps our own teaching fresh and is a well we can always return to for inspiration.

We teach and model, explicitly and implicitly, by working through the challenges and celebrating the rewards of our own mindfulness practice. Will our children be more inspired if we tell them that mindfulness has made us more creative, calm, concentrated, and compassionate, or if we show them our wise actions and compassionate interactions? Will the kids be more engaged in a practice if we press play on a meditation CD and promptly start in on our own chores and paperwork, or if we sit down and share practice together?

As you deepen your own mindfulness practice, you will also discover not only that your confidence increases, but that new insights and creative ideas for sharing mindfulness will arise, new wisdom for handling challenging situations will become clear, and even new practices and adaptations of practices may come to mind.

CHAPTER 5

visualizing mindfulness
harnessing the imagination

The man who has no imagination
Stands on earth.
He has no wings,
He cannot fly.

MUHAMMAD ALI, in *Muhammad Ali In Fighter's Heaven*
by Victor Bockris

We make mindfulness practice fun and kid-friendly by integrating it into play, games, stories, arts, visualization, or movement—all the natural ways children learn and explore the world. There is growing research on the importance of play. (In fact, another child mindfulness teacher told me that she was recently asked, "Is play the new mindfulness?") Visualization is playing with the imagination, a powerful resource for both children and adults.

Education researchers Elena Bodrova and Deborah Leong have worked on the wonderful "Tools of the Mind" executive function curriculum inspired by the work of child development and play expert Lev Vygotsky.[1] In a simple test, he instructed four-year-olds to stand still for as long they could. This was about as effective as you might imagine: after just a few minutes, most kids were on to the next thing, already giving up. But when they were asked first to imagine themselves as guards at a factory, they could, on average, stand still for about four times as long. Vygotsky found that children playing or acting out a scene can control impulses, retain their attention, and remain on task far more effectively than when they're just told to do these things.

We all know the power of the imagination in the abstract, but consider the fact that it can quadruple attention span and suppress impulsivity. Knowing this, how can you imagine using imagination with the children in your life? Maybe the Soviet-era idea of guarding a factory doesn't sound so inspirational, but what about knights at a castle or a model posing in a new dress? For posture, we can ask kids to sit up tall and regally, like a king or queen, or ask them to imagine an invisible string attached to the top of their head.

Visualization and guided imagery practices build on Vygotsky's work and give the mind an easy place to rest. They also tap into the power of metaphor.

The Power of Metaphor

The concept of mindfulness is abstract, which is why for centuries teachers have used metaphors. Jon Kabat-Zinn uses the images of sitting solid like a mountain or lying flat and reflective like a lake in mindfulness practices. Yoga and movement practices are full of imagery and metaphor, as we stretch our bodies into the shapes of powerful animals. Metaphor works like poetry, what a friend of mine calls "limbic language." Neuroscience research shows that metaphor activates the sensory part of the brain, not just the language part; it gives us a felt sense of an abstract concept.[2]

One of my favorite mindfulness images, probably because of my own positive associations, is that of thoughts as leaves floating down a river or mountain stream. The idea is to watch the thoughts, but not get caught in the stream. If you do, simply pull yourself out. As not every kid has experienced a mountain stream, another metaphor might make more sense, depending on your child's interests, background, and experiences.

Below is a brief list of metaphors I have compiled from other therapists and meditation teachers. You can try envisioning thoughts as:

- being carried gently downstream on leaves, some moving
  fast, some stuck swirling in place

- items being carried past on a conveyor belt

- words or pictures marked on parade floats, or signs carried
  by marchers in a parade

- autumn leaves falling from trees and landing softly on an
  empty, accepting blanket of consciousness

- being highlighted, one by one, as a karaoke video
  highlights lyrics

- bubbles floating past in the air

- clouds forming and unforming, passing by against the
  blue sky

- scenery passing by the windows of a train

- animals, such as happy and sad fish swimming through the
  water in an aquarium, or angry and peaceful birds flying by

- traffic seen from high above; some thoughts may be big
  buses that cannot stop, others may be motorcycles zipping
  from lane to lane, and still others may be stuck on the side
  of the road

- scenes and characters in a movie

- leaves blowing across your path

- raindrops hitting a windshield before being wiped away

- specks of dust floating in a ray of sunlight

Metaphors for remaining present and aware in the face of challenges include:

- You are watching the cars of a roller coaster or carnival ride go by, with ups and downs, twists and turns, but you're not climbing on board.

- You are throwing a stone into a pond and watching the ripples it makes, but not getting bounced around them.

- You are a bee flitting from flower to flower, and you return back to the hive with sweet new insights from the world.

Which metaphors stand out and speak to you? Which might work for the children in your life? Are there others you can use or have used? Can you think of a way to explore these images with young people, perhaps in a meditation, art, or writing project?

How to Use Visualization Practices

All the practices in this chapter use imagery as the anchor of attention. The scripts can be adapted for each particular kid, plugging in some of the examples above. (For more on adapting practices, see chapter 12.) You can read them aloud, improvise, or even record them for your kids to listen to on their digital devices. I suggest reading them through once or twice before sharing them aloud.

Here are some tips for sharing visualizations with kids:

- Anxious or perfectionist kids might worry about getting the "right" lake, tree, or other image you're asking them to visualize, or they may have trouble settling on an image.

They may need a prompt like a short video or photo, or they might enjoy a chance to draw their image before doing the visualization.

- Some kids may not have a positive association with the image you're asking them to visualize or be able to picture a certain image. Letting them choose their own imagery can help.

- Some kids may take longer to settle on an image. Don't rush them. You can ask for a signal, like raising a finger, to let you know they've got their image.

- Reminding kids at the beginning and throughout what to do if their mind wanders lets kids know that it is normal for their mind to wander.

- Drop in the sentence, "If your mind wanders off, just follow your breath back to the image or the still point between the breaths," if you see squirming or sense distraction.

- It is helpful to have some kind of reminder at the end telling kids that they can reconnect with the experience at any time later. This reminder will help them integrate the practice into their life.

TREE PRACTICE

An ancient tree, strong yet flexible, is to me the perfect metaphor for confidence and perseverance in the face of change or challenge. I use this Tree Practice with kids who are struggling with confidence or fearful of standing their ground against bullies of any size. This takes about five minutes, which you can extend or shorten to suit your kid's needs and attention span. It is inspired by Jon Kabat-Zinn's Lake Meditation.

Start by standing with your feet about hip width apart, arms resting at your sides. Take a few deep breaths, perhaps shrugging your shoulders, and allow your eyes to gently close.

Bring your awareness to your feet. Imagine that the soles of your feet have roots reaching deep into the earth. From your feet upward, feel a sense of growing and reaching up, like a beautiful, power-ful, and ancient tree. With each breath, feel more strongly rooted in the earth and, at the same time, tall and strong.

Now bring to mind a tree. You can pick any kind of tree you like, from your experience or your imagi-nation, from a book or a movie. A tree that changes with the seasons will work best.

Like you, this tree stands tall wherever it is rooted. It just watches as the days pass, on some days grow-ing up toward the bright sun in the blue sky, and at night, bathing in the light of the moon. Through it all, the tree stands solid as the world around it changes.

The weather may change. Drenching rain and cracking thunderstorms may soak the tree and nour-ish its roots. Winds may whip and the branches may bend, but they never break.

On other days, the hot sun gives energy to the leaves and branches. Through it all, the tree remains standing, reaching confidently upward.

As days and nights pass, summertime turns to fall, and the days grow shorter. The temperature drops, but the tree stands. Leaves begin to dry, changing from bright green to yellow and deeper oranges and reds. Yet the roots go deep, and the branches still reach high. Harsh, cold winds may blow, the tree may sway, and some leaves may blow away, but the tree holds firm. Some part deep inside remains still and calm.

Eventually, the leaves let go of the tree, and the tree lets them go. The leaves blow away, and winter surrounds the tree. The drab landscape and gray skies do not move the tree. Winter storms batter the tree with ice and snow, and branches rustle in the wind but never break.

Gradually winter fades. As days lengthen, blue skies return, and the first green buds return to the branches. The branches sway gently against the sky in the spring breeze, but the roots hold firm. The tree reaches high into the sky, relaxing in the sunlight as the leaves return.

Like the tree, you can stand tall, rooted in the face of whatever arises. Some days may be bleak and gray. Others may appear stormy and overwhelming. And yet, like the tree, you can remain still at your core, bending without breaking, growing deeper down and higher up with each day that passes.

Take a few more breaths down into your roots, feeling your confidence grow, and then gradually open your eyes and bring your awareness back into the room.

CLOUDS IN THE SKY

This practice was inspired by a similar practice that Lizabeth Roemer and Susan M. Orsillo share in their book *The Mindful Way Through Anxiety.*[3] You can make it longer by repeating a few instructions and spacing out the prompts.

Take a moment to find a comfortable posture; you can stand, sit, or lie down. When you feel comfortable, allow your eyes to close.

Imagine yourself in a beautiful place—perhaps the beach, a wide open field, or somewhere in the mountains. Maybe this is a place you know, or one that exists in a movie or book, or one that exists in your imagination.

Looking up, you can see a wide blue sky, with just a few puffy white clouds drifting past.

Notice thoughts going past in your mind. As you notice each thought, see if you can visualize it shrinking, and then place it on a passing cloud as it floats by.

You might notice that some clouds get stuck or move slowly, others sail by more quickly on the air currents, and some change their shape or size. But all of them eventually pass and drift away in the sky. If they get stuck, you can even try breathing out to gently push the clouds onward.

Take time to just notice your thoughts and feelings, placing them on a cloud and letting them drift away on your breath.

You may find yourself caught in the clouds from time to time, floating with the thoughts, caught up in the clouds themselves. If this happens, just notice which thought pulled you in, bring yourself back to that beautiful place with the view, breathe the clouds away, and return to watching again.

Take time to watch your thoughts and feelings, big and small, happy and sad, as they rest on the clouds and eventually float away.

As you finish, remember that all your thoughts and feelings will eventually pass. Allow your eyes to open.

You can play around with the images in the script above to shift the metaphor to a river with thoughts floating by, to something like watching traffic from an overpass, or animals migrating across the Serengeti. Over time, certain metaphors begin to stick with particular kids, and become part of our common language: "My thoughts are stuck in a depression whirlpool on the side of the river," or, "I put my math worries on a cloud and let them float away."

THE STONE IN THE LAKE

My patient Julie, who had had a childhood illness, was anxious about getting in touch with her body. This practice allowed her to set an anchor in the stillness of her body, without asking her to remain there for a longer body-based practice. For kids who feel uncentered or unbalanced, this can be a very grounding practice. In my office, I have a small collection of smooth stones from beaches and mountains I've traveled to. Julie took one to keep in her pocket, so that she can touch and be reminded of the stone in the lake.

This practice takes its inspiration from similar imagery by Jon Kabat-Zinn and Amy Saltzman.

Sit or lie down and find a comfortable, sustainable posture.

Bring your attention to your breath. Connect with the still point where the in-breath has paused just before it rises back up as the out-breath. Do this again for the next three breaths.

If your mind wanders off during the following instructions, just follow your breath back to the still point between the breaths.

Now, imagine a beautiful lake, preferably one in a climate with four seasons. This can be a lake you've visited and liked, or it can be one you've seen in a photo or a movie or read about in a book, or maybe just one you imagine.

(Pause. Perhaps ask the participant to give you a silent signal—a raised hand, a nod—to let you know when they've found their image.)

On the next in-breath, imagine that someone has tossed a pebble into the center of the lake. Follow the stone downward as you follow the breath downward, past the surface. Follow it down to where it rests and is held by the soft bottom of the lake. There it can remain still and undisturbed by the lake water or the world around.

At the surface, the lake reflects the world around it. On a summer's day, the lake may reflect blue skies and bright green trees, and echo with sounds of life. Hour by hour, the world and its reflection may look different, as the bright hues of sunset color the surface, giving way to a reflection of the stars and moon above. And all the while, the stone remains deep below—still, quiet, and undisturbed.

The days pass—some bringing blue skies, some clouds and storms. The surface of the lake may ripple as rain beats down, or the wind may cause swells on the surface. Yet below the surface there is stillness.

The days shorten as summer fades and fall begins. The reflection of green trees turns to gold, orange, and scarlet as the leaves begin to turn and the air grows colder. And yet, underneath, the stone remains still.

Even as the occasional autumn leaf drifts down to the bottom of the lake next to the stone, it remains unmoved, resting on the bottom.

The trees eventually become bare, and the sky whitens as winter sets in. Ice sheets form, snow falls. The surface of the lake turns to ice, and the ice is buried in snow. Foggy days or snowy blizzards make the lake hard to see. And yet the stone on the sandy bottom remains in its place.

As winter fades, the snow and ice melt. The cold water seeps down to the stone, but does not disturb its rest.

Trees begin to blossom and birds come back. Signs of life and color return with springtime. Through it all, the stone remains still.

We are like the lake. The world around us changes, our own surface changes, and even our outward appearance changes. But we always have the stillness, like the stone, resting within. The world may touch us, just as the cold water or leaf touches the stone, but it need not move us.

> You can always connect with this stillness below the surface by touching it with the bottom of your in-breath, by feeling your feet connecting with the ground, or even by touching a stone in your pocket.
>
> As you bring your awareness back to the world around you, maintain your connection to the stillness within. And know you can always return to it.

Other imagery can be substituted for the lake. In *Sitting Together,* Susan Pollak, Thomas Pedulla, and Ronald Siegel suggest the image of an anchor dropping into the sea to secure a boat drifting and bobbing on the water.[4] Another image you might try is that of a floating hot air balloon tethered to the ground. Use your imagination, use the kid's imagination and experience, and have fun with it.

THE GLITTER JAR

Children, especially struggling ones, tend to *act* out their difficulties rather than share them in words. We adults are often only marginally better. When words are unavailable, it helps to find other ways to demonstrate the connection between thoughts, feelings, and behaviors.

A snow globe or glitter jar is one of the most powerful visual metaphors for that connection; it illustrates how mindfulness—the cultivation of stillness in the face of the swirling chaos of life—affects us. In this practice, you can actually make a glitter jar. At first I used to do this practice only with young kids, but I've since found that even teens enjoy it.

You can use a mason jar, a spice jar, or even a plastic water bottle for this practice. Be sure to use glitter that sinks rather than floats. Adding some glycerin to the water slows down the fall of the glitter.

Fill the jar to the top with water. Have your children pick three colors of glitter: one to represent thoughts, one to represent feelings, and one to represent behaviors (or "urges to do things"). Drop a few pinches of each color glitter into the water, which represents their mind, and maybe a few drops of food coloring. Seal the jar with its lid or duct tape.

Ask the children what kinds of things will make the glitter in the jar swirl. Encourage answers that reflect distressing events (fights with siblings, losing in sports) and positive ones (getting a good grade, making a new friend), events in the foreground (sick siblings) and events in the background (scary stories on the news). With each event they name, swirl and turn the jar, demonstrating how it becomes difficult to keep track and see clearly what our thoughts, feelings, and urges are.

Your script can go something like this:

The jar is like our mind, and each color of glitter represents something different in our mind.

Let's put in red for thoughts, gold for feelings, and silver for urges to do things. *(Pour in a little bit of glitter with each comment.)*

Now we seal up the jar. *(Put the lid on the jar and seal it.)* Then we start our day.

We wake up, and things are pretty settled. We can see that clearly. *(Show how all the glitter has settled on the bottom of the jar.)*

But pretty soon, things start swirling around. Maybe we are running late *(swirl the jar)*. Our big sister eats the last pancake for breakfast, and it leads to a fight *(shake the jar)*. We hear scary things on the news in the car ride to school *(swirl the jar)*. We get to school, and find out we aced the test *(shake the jar)*.

Now it's only a few minutes into the school day, and we can't see clearly because all of our thoughts and feelings and urges are getting in the way.

So what is the one thing we can do to get the glitter to settle and see clearly again?

Be still. That's right!

And what happens when we are still? That's right—we can see clearly again.

There is also no way to rush being still. We can't push all the glitter down to the bottom. We just have to watch and wait. No amount of effort will make it settle sooner.

When things become clear, we'll know the wise next thing to do. In fact, that's one definition of wisdom: seeing things as they are and choosing how to act.

While we wait, does the glitter go away? No, it stays at the bottom. Our thoughts and feelings and urges are still in our minds, but they are no longer in our way, clouding our vision.

There are many variations of this practice, depending on what you want to emphasize. My colleague Jan Mooney, who often works with groups of kids, uses a giant jar that all the kids can add glitter to. Each color represents different feelings the kids have. Other variations include using a few plastic beads, which float, to represent behaviors and watching until the behaviors separate from thoughts and feelings. Kids can also try to focus on just one color, or one piece of glitter until it settles, or all of them.

A finished glitter jar can serve as a visual timer for other practices, such as breathing practices. For example, you can shake the jar and say, "Let's do some mindful breaths until the glitter settles." Some families use the jar as a "calm-down jar," to mark and measure calm-down time. Ideally, the entire family can use the calm-down jar together when there is a conflict: "We are all upset with lots of thoughts and feelings right now. So let's all take a break until the glitter in the calm-down jar has settled and then start talking again." There are even a few glitter jar and snow-globe smartphone apps, which one kid I work with just loves.

One particularly sharp student of mine pointed out that you could just take a filter and make the jar clear again. He had a point, and it wasn't until I was driving home that I came up with the comeback: "We actually don't want to get rid of the thoughts and feelings and urges. We just want them out of the way so they don't prevent us from seeing clearly."

SETTLING PRACTICE

We too sometimes need to settle—in our minds and in our bodies. Settling the mind can start with settling in our bodies. This practice was inspired by meditation teacher Tara Brach's "Touchpoints" practice.

Sit down and find a comfortable, upright posture. Sit with a feeling of lifting up through your chest and head, and a feeling of gravity weighing down through your legs and feet.

Allow your eyes to close, or if it feels more comfortable, allow them to rest on the floor in front of you.

Now become aware of the sensations of settling. First be aware of your breath settling into a natural rhythm.

Starting with the top of your head, feel the sensations of the hair settling on your head, and maybe also settling on your neck and shoulders.

Bring your awareness to your eyelids, allowing the upper lids to come to rest on the lower lids—settled, relaxed, and still.

Let part or all of your upper lip settle on your lower lip. Allow your tongue to rest on the floor of your mouth. Let the natural forces of gravity do their work as you bring awareness to these points of contact and settling.

Feel your head and skull resting on your spine.

Feel your organs inside settling, resting, but still held by your body.

Bring awareness to your arms and hands, feeling the sensations where they rest at your side or settle on your legs.

Notice and feel the sensation where your seat and thighs meet the chair, and settle in, your thighs gently pushing into the surface underneath you. Let gravity keep you stable and still.

Notice the sensations of your feet in your shoes or on the floor.

With your whole body settled, now allow your thoughts to settle down as well.

If you like, take a moment to scan your body and find one settled point that is most noticeable. Remember that you can always come back to that point, any time of day, when you are sitting in your chair or on the ground.

Still aware of feeling settled, allow your eyes to open, and notice if you see the world more clearly.

∪

There are many images that can act as an anchor. Consider what makes sense in terms of what your kid knows, what they like, and what will resonate with them as you guide them through a practice grounded in visualization.

CHAPTER 6

mind the body

body-based
mindfulness practices

There is more sagacity in thy body than in thy best wisdom.

FRIEDRICH NIETZCHE, *Thus Spake Zarathustra*,
translated by Thomas Common

⋃

In traditional texts, there are four foundations of mindfulness. The first is mindfulness of body. There are many good reasons to start with the body. For one thing, the body is easier to pay attention to than thoughts, mental events, emotions, or even the breath. The body is the seat of our five perceptual senses, which anchor us in the present, and is the source of our felt emotions. Eastern psychology suggests that emotions arise in the body before reaching the mind, which creates suffering out of the pain and discomfort. (Interestingly, many Asian languages, even those of Buddhist cultures such as Tibetan, do not have a word for "emotion." Instead they refer to "thought sensations.") Western science is finally catching up. A Finnish study of over seven hundred people from around the world asked people to identify where in the body they felt emotions.[1] The researchers found that across cultures, the physical experience of emotions is largely the same, with similar sensations arising in the same parts of the body, mostly in the trunk, in response to a particular emotion. When we tune into the body, it offers up information about our emotional state.

The body can act as an early warning system for stress, and by coming to know their bodies mindfully, kids learn to care for themselves before becoming overwhelmed, potentially saving them and everyone around them from later suffering. Identifying and describing the experience of their body is usually easier for kids than describing the emotional world of their mind, for which they may not yet have language. The creators of Mindfulness-Based Cognitive Therapy (MBCT) point out that we naturally describe emotions in the body.[2] Consider some common idiomatic expressions in English: "I feel hot under the collar," "There are butterflies in my stomach," "My heart swelled with love when I saw her across the room." All describe emotional experiences (anger, anxiety, and love) as physical sensations. It stands to reason that paying deeper attention to the body will bring deeper, more nuanced understanding of emotional experiences and responses. And while thoughts in our mind may be stuck in the past or racing to the future, our body and our five senses always remain anchored in the present.

Yet we live in a culture which fosters disconnection from the body, blocking that healthy mind–body integration. This disconnect exacerbates difficulties in learning, health, and mental health among all age groups. Many physical, mental, and even learning disorders can be understood as a lack of integration between mind and body. In the West, we have been operating under the assumption of a mind–body split since the seventeenth century, when René Descartes posited a mind–body duality that does not reflect the reality that mind and body are one. We are raised with strong cultural messages that revere the power of cognition. While politicians promote the "decade of the brain," social scientists attempt to explain all behavior as the result of chemical imbalances in the brain.

Many factors interrupt healthy mind–body integration. The shame of trauma—recent or distant, whether caused by illness, accident, abuse, or neglect—causes many children to disconnect from their bodily experiences. Getting in touch with their bodies, or parts of their bodies, is frightening. Media messages about body image further complicate things, particularly for girls and women, but increasingly for boys and men. Anxiety reactions are a disorder of the flight response; anger problems, the fight response; and depression, the freeze/submit response, as explored in chapter 1. Escaping, avoiding, or ignoring the body is a natural defense against these feelings. Substance abuse, even if it never reaches the level of addiction, severs the mind–body connection and abuses both the body and mind. Self-harming behaviors, such as cutting, do the same. Even just mindless eating, such as eating while we're reading or watching TV rather than paying attention to what we eat, distracts us from hearing the body's wise messages about what it truly needs.

The consequences of this mind–body disconnect are profound. When we are out of touch with our bodies, we don't get the information we need for healthy emotional and cognitive functioning. A lack of body awareness leads to difficulty identifying emotional states. This, in turn, means that many children don't know what to do with strong emotions or urges that arise first in the body. Without recognizing them, they struggle to express these feelings verbally or in other appropriate ways. When they can't, they act out in ways that, over time, become hardwired habits. A lack of ability to regulate responses to strong emotions leads to further avoidance. Over time, as strong emotions arise (whether in the family setting, the classroom, therapy, or the world), a child's bandwidth for emotional processing becomes smaller and smaller, until they are unable to learn in the classroom or engage in productive conversation with others. And when that child cannot be present with themselves, they cannot be present in relationships with others, including in friendships with peers, securely attached relationships with caregivers, and working relationships with teachers, therapists, or other professionals. This inability to be present with others leads to further isolation.

Sharon Salzberg explains that we can't deal with an emotion when we're consumed by it or fighting it; first we must learn to recognize it, and the easiest way to do that is by recognizing it in the body. We can teach emotional awareness and emotional intelligence by teaching mindfulness of the body's signals. When children recognize emotions early on in the laboratory of their own body, those emotions lose their power to hijack the brain.

Research by psychotherapists Eugene Gendlin and Carl Rogers found that the people who improved most in therapy after a year were the ones who identified emotions in their bodies.[3] In the Zen tradition and in kung fu, there is a notion that the whole body is involved in seeking answers and making meaning. Over time, this whole-body experience transforms our relationship to the world and people around us, which then reinforces the positive changes. Just as we can turn the mind into an ally, we can turn the body into an ally as well. This means building greater awareness and ultimately tolerance for emotional content in life. Doing so reconnects and reintegrates the natural mind–body connection that has been lost over time, so that each component learns from and works with the other to regulate and heal our entire system.

Body-based mindfulness practices reintegrate and recalibrate the mind–body system, restoring it to its optimal settings. Through mindfulness-of-body practices, kids learn that physical sensations, both comfortable and uncomfortable, arise and pass, and that emotional content too will arise and pass with time, without us having to react to it.

NAME AND TAME IT

There's an old saying in psychotherapy: "Name it and tame it." This means that when we recognize emotions, they become less powerful. When participants in an experiment were connected to an fMRI and asked to label emotions on faces they were shown, their amygdala (the brain's alarm system) calmed down as they named the emotions, and the prefrontal cortex (higher-order thinking) activated. Just the act of naming the emotion, as we often do in mindfulness practice, allowed them to pause and respond with forethought rather than react with emotion. The contrast was even more apparent in participants who ranked high on a scale of mindfulness.[4]

MIND-BODY GO!

To take a quick moment to notice sensations in your body and associated thoughts, Susan Kaiser Greenland recommends a game she calls Mind–Body Go! It is about as straightforward as it sounds. In a group setting, everyone takes a turn identifying one feeling in the body and one feeling in the mind, but quickly and without thinking first. For example, "I feel tight in the body, stressed in my mind," or, "My body feels tired, and my mind feels sad." Participants can sit in a circle with each person offering an answer in turn, or they can offer their answers at random, popcorn style.

ICE, ICE BABY

This fun group activity uses ice cubes to explore the impermanence of mental and physical discomfort and our emotional response to it. The supplies you will need are cups, ice cubes, and napkins or paper towels.

Hand each participant a paper towel and a cup containing an ice cube. While you're still passing out the ice, invite them to notice the physical and emotional aspects of both waiting and curiosity.

Once everyone has an ice cube, explain that everyone will hold the ice in their hand for one minute. Then ask them for their first reaction to hearing what is about to happen. Excitement? Fear? Laughter?

Instruct everyone to hold their ice cube in one hand. Tell them to just notice the sensations of holding the ice: What do you notice physically in your hand as you focus on the sensation? Where does your mind tend to go? What emotions are you feeling? What urges are you noticing? What do you want to do, and how do you deal with that urge?

After one minute, or when the ice has melted, signal the end of the session and allow the participants to clean up. Then ask for responses to the activity.

At the end of the exercise, discussion questions can be used to pull out different insights, depending on the objective of the exercise. The following questions explore the ways we respond to discomfort and dislike:

- How did you feel? Frustrated? Scared? Excited *(maybe on a hot day)*? Annoyed? Something else? What happened if you focused on the sensation, or if you focused on something else?

- What were the urges? Did you want to show off, laugh, drop the ice, distract yourself?

- How did you get through the discomfort? Did you ignore it? Did you focus on something else?

- What did you notice about how you deal with discomfort or dislike?

- Would you feel or act differently if you were alone, if you were around different people, or if the temperature in the room were different?

- Was it harder or easier to hold the ice when you knew you'd be holding the ice for just one minute? How would your feeling change if I told you to hold it as long as possible?

The central lessons that usually emerge include recognizing and tolerating feelings and urges and seeing them as impermanent, as well as recognizing reactions to discomfort. This exercise also offers lessons in impermanence, as whatever we do, the ice cube will eventually melt anyway.

Interoception: Does "Wise Mind" Actually Live in the Body?

By teaching young people mindfulness of body, we teach intuitive emotional awareness that will serve them well in the long run. *Interoception* means sensing from within—essentially, using the body as a source of information. We can use the information we sense internally in addition to the external information we receive via our perceptual organs (exteroception) to make decisions, rather than just relying on highly charged emotional signals from the brain.

We know that the nervous system is spread throughout the body. In fact, some of our most important intuitive neural networks, which appear to be linked to the storage of our core values, are located near the heart and near the intestines. Scientific research backs up the idea that when we say "listen to your heart" or "go with your gut," we're being more than just metaphorical. We get signals worth listening to from these parts of the body.

Dialectical Behavioral Therapy, a modality developed recently by psychologist Marsha Linehan, encourages participants to find their "wise mind"—the balance between a sometimes overly logical "reason mind" and a potentially impulsive "emotion mind." The emotion mind represents the primitive limbic system, and the reason mind represents the refined prefrontal lobes. But new research suggests that the wise mind, our internal compass, might be located within our bodies, in our heart and gut. Tuning into our body awareness helps us to access wisdom beyond what our brains and emotions can offer. The body has its own answers, especially to complicated problems. A famous proverb, often attributed to Albert Einstein, says that we can't solve problems by using the same kind of thinking we used when we created them. To me, that means using the body, not just the brain, as in the Decision Practice in chapter 3.

PERSONAL SPACE PRACTICE

My friend and colleague Joan Klagsbrun, a clinical psychologist, suggests the following practice for helping kids recognize the body's innate wisdom about comfort and discomfort, boundaries, and personal space. It demonstrates the body's intuitive wisdom and ability to detect discomfort, which we don't always notice, especially when we're distracted.

Stand two kids about fifteen feet apart. Instruct both to focus on sensations in their bodies.

Now ask one to slowly walk toward the other. Ask the standing child to focus on sensations in their gut and notice when the other person gets too close. If they pay close attention, they will likely get a signal from their body, usually a tensing in the gut. At that point, they can raise their hand to signal "stop."

This practice can be integrated into the walking meditations discussed in the next chapter, and it can lead to discussions about boundaries, personal space, and listening to our bodies. The idea of comfortable distance will vary across individuals and across cultures. (We Americans often want more personal space than people from other countries do.)

THE IMPORTANCE OF BODY LANGUAGE

Body awareness is important not just for kids, but also in our own work with them. The more we adults are disconnected from our bodily and emotional experience, the less securely we can form attachments as parents or caregivers, and the more we will sow feelings of mistrust and create an environment unfriendly to growth and learning. How aware we are of our body language can also make a significant difference in what we communicate to ourselves and the world. Research shows that reading body language can even predict how often a doctor gets sued or how likely a couple is to break up.[5]

ADAPTED BODY SCAN

The body scan, a longer activity used by Jon Kabat-Zinn in his MBSR program, is a good practice for teaching body awareness.

Many parents have found their kids enjoy body scans, especially when combined with some progressive muscle relaxation. The basic structure is to sweep awareness up the body, noticing sensations and related emotions in various parts of the body. You can also start with sensations at the outside of the body and move inward. Scripts can be found in my previous book, *Child's Mind,* or in Kabat-Zinn's *Full Catastrophe Living.*[6]

The body scan included in MBSR is a long practice, and it may not be right in some settings or for some young people. I usually work one-on-one with kids, and I've found that some kids are not comfortable lying on my couch and closing their eyes while I guide them through such a practice. Instead, I do a variation with them, in which we name and share our experiences back and forth. You can also do this practice with a larger group, having participants take turns sharing their sensations out loud. Or you can have them write down what they experience, or draw it.

Start the scan from the bottom of the body and move upward. First scan the lower body, then the torso, and then the upper body. Participants can take turns wondering what each part of the body feels like, what it could be telling them, and what they can do. For example, "My legs feel twitchy. They are like that when I'm nervous or excited. I think I must be nervous, so I'll focus on breathing into the bottoms of my feet to see if that calms me down." This can open up conversation about how we deal with feelings, likes and dislikes, and ways we can respond to them. Discussing how we choose to respond is working with the "about-to moment" that meditation teacher Joseph Goldstein talks about—the moment before we react impulsively. Identifying this about-to moment is where emotional awareness begins, especially with younger kids.

If kids feel nothing during this practice, which is certainly possible, identifying contrasts like hot or cold, moisture or dryness, sore or relaxed, and sensations inside the body versus on the surface can all stimulate a little more awareness without leading kids too much.

Mindful Eating

One cannot think well, love well, sleep well, if one has not dined well.

VIRGINIA WOOLF, *A Room of One's Own*

As living beings, we have to eat. In our culture, eating has become something most of us do mind*less*ly, with little thought or attention, or it has become an overthought activity, loaded with complicated ideas about food and bodies, most of which are perpetuated by the media. But eating can offer an opportunity for us to connect with the moment, with our experience, with others, and with the planet. By bringing mindfulness to our body through eating, we can bring self-care to something that may otherwise feel like self-indulgence.

In our culture, we often confuse self-care and self-indulgence, and we pass that down to our kids. We deny ourselves healthy self-care, complaining that there is no time to enjoy a meal, meditate, or spend quality time with the people we love, and sometimes labeling these activities frivolous self-indulgence. At the same time, we get messages from the media that over-indulging in shopping, eating, drinking, screen time, and other distractions are self-care.

Fresh out of college, I was working in a group home. There was a lot of talk from the higher-ups about the need for self-care in such a high-stress job. The staff, meanwhile, joked about the sixteen ounces of self-care that were waiting at the bar after the shift was over—a clear confusion of self-indulgence and self-care. Many of us who work hard mentally, emotionally, and physically struggle with maintaining good habits at the end of the day and fall on the side of self-indulgence, even when we know it's not a healthy long-term solution.

Working on a college campus, and even with younger kids, I see clearly the confusion and conflation of self-care and self-indulgence. Self-care is not mindlessly using substances or mindlessly playing video games, depending on your age. While many people do have good everyday habits, when stressed out, their self-care shortcut may be eating a pint of ice cream, spending hours in bed, or watching hours of streaming television, rather than engaging in healthier behaviors. It's not that self-indulgence is always bad; mindfully indulging in sensory pleasures, from time to time, can be an excellent form of self-care. The difficulty is finding a balance between self-care and self-indulgence and not confusing the two, for ourselves or for our kids.

There are healthy ways to combine self-care and self-indulgence. I like to do this with food. Mindfully eating fresh fruit, chocolate, ice cream, or other treats can be a wonderful way to access the present moment and offer valuable lessons in impermanence, desire, urges, and body awareness, as well as the complexities and nuances of life.

One of the goals of mindful living is to bring awareness to all aspects of daily life—breathing, moving, playing, and even eating. Like breathing or movement, eating is a daily activity we often do automatically, giving little thought to the experience. Preparing and eating food can be done with deliberate, mindful attention to all of the senses. Slowing down and bringing awareness to our bodies and the food we consume may wake some of us up to how healthy our food is and how much of it we really need. Mindful eating can also be a way of reminding ourselves how food connects us to others, to the culture and history of our ancestors, to the seasons and to caring for the earth, and ultimately to everything in the universe. When we see deeply how interconnected we are with everything, our wisdom and our compassion both grow stronger.

Thich Nhat Hanh calls our interconnection with all things *interbeing*. Though he uses the example of paper instead of food, his description of interbeing shows just how vast and intricate our interconnection is:

> If you are a poet, you will see clearly that there is a cloud
> floating in this sheet of paper. Without a cloud, there
> will be no rain; without rain, the trees cannot grow;
> and without trees, we cannot make paper. The cloud is
> essential for the paper to exist. If the cloud is not here,
> the sheet of paper cannot be here either. So we can say
> that the cloud and the paper *inter-are*. "Interbeing" is a
> word that is not in the dictionary yet, but if we combine
> the prefix "inter" with the verb "to be," we have a new

verb, inter-be. So we can say that the cloud and the sheet of paper *inter-are*.

If we look into this sheet of paper even more deeply, we can see the sunshine in it. If the sunshine is not there, the forest cannot grow. In fact, nothing can grow. Even we cannot grow without sunshine. And so, we know that the sunshine is also in this sheet of paper. The paper and the sunshine inter-are. And if we continue to look, we can see the logger who cut the tree and brought it to the mill to be transformed into paper. And we see the wheat. We know the logger cannot exist without his daily bread, and therefore, the wheat that became his bread is also in this sheet of paper. And the logger's father and mother are in it too. When we look in this way, we see that without all of these things, this sheet of paper cannot exist.

Looking even more deeply, we can see we are in it too. This is not difficult to see, because when we look at a sheet of paper, the sheet of paper is part of our perception. Your mind is in here and mine is also. So we can say that everything is in here with this sheet of paper. You cannot point out one thing that is not here—time, space, the Earth, the rain, the minerals in the soil, the sunshine, the cloud, the river, the heat. Everything co-exists with this sheet of paper. That is why I think the word "inter-be" should be in the dictionary. "To be" is to inter-be. You cannot just be by yourself alone. You have to inter-be with every other thing. This sheet of paper is, because everything else is.[7]

INTRODUCING KIDS TO MINDFUL EATING

When introducing kids to the practice of mindful eating, it can help to start with a fun food. Chocolate, dark or milk, can be both bitter and sweet and has far more flavors than many of us realize are in there. Strong-tasting foods, be they strong mints like Altoids, sour lemon candies, or atomic fireballs, can provoke strong emotions, which can be opportunities for conversations and lessons in tolerating discomfort as we watch it arise and pass. You can also try to teach patience and noticing urges by eating hard candies or lollipops and trying not to bite them. Other teachers use berries, with sweet flesh and bitter seeds. Or you can ask kids to notice their reactions to eating unpleasant foods to explore the concepts of aversion and dislike. My friend, teacher Susan Mordecai, used raisins one week and grapes the next in a mindful eating practice with kids. She noticed that many kids didn't even know that they are the same fruit until they really paid attention and tasted the grape. Other dried fruit, or a selection of mixed dried fruit or trail mix, can be more interesting than a raisin. Another option is a fruit that takes time to peel and has many sensory components to notice as you do, like a clementine.

The following practice script was inspired by similar scripts in the MBSR program, MBCT, and the Mindfulness in Schools Project. It includes my own additions. You will likely need to adapt it, depending on your kid's age, attention span, experience, and what they are eating.

If I tell you I've brought you something, what happens? What do you notice in your mind and body?

And if I say I've brought you something to eat, what happens? What do you notice in your mind and body?

What if I told you I've brought you chocolate? (Substitute the name of whatever food you are using.)

Just notice how your mind and body start to respond to those words as I share this food with you. Please don't eat it yet. Just hold it in your hands.

What is it like in your mind and body as you wait?

Now, I'd like you to just look at this food with fresh eyes, mindful eyes, as if you've never seen anything like this before, even though you have.

And if doing this feels strange or silly, just notice that and set aside those thoughts for the next couple of minutes.

Now, take a moment to consider the journey this food took to arrive in your hands. Think about how it came from my hands, my car, the store, the people that brought it from the farm or factory to the store, all the way to your hand and soon to your mouth. And consider everything it took to make this: the sunlight to grow the ingredients, the rainwater, the things that made up the packaging. All of these are a part of this too—all the people and places and elements are part of this being here now in your hands.

Perhaps you can imagine those people and places in this food.

Start to explore this with your senses.

First, explore the visual sense, carefully turning this food around in your hand and examining it in the light.

Close your eyes and feel it, noticing texture and temperature against the skin of your hand and fingers, feeling its weight as it rests in your palm.

Keeping your eyes closed, raise it to one ear and then the other. Yes, listen to it, especially as you move it in your fingers.

Now bring it under your nose. First, just breathe in through your nose. Notice all that happens as you breathe in—how your body responds, your mouth and stomach—and also how your mind responds with thoughts and feelings and memories.

Now bring the food away from your nose.

(If the food is wrapped or has a peel: Unwrap/unpeel the food. As you do, listen to all the sounds of unwrapping and notice what happens with your other senses as well. Notice again the smells, as well as the emotions that come up for you.)

Lift the food to your lips and hold it there, but don't take a bite yet. Notice the sensations in your mouth and body. Also observe the thoughts, feelings, and urges in your mind and body. What is your stomach telling you, or your mouth asking you?

Now take the smallest bite you can. Watch what the mind does and what the body does—your stomach and your saliva, your thoughts and feelings, your memories and associations.

Wait a moment for these sensations to fade. Then close your eyes and place the food on your tongue without moving it. For now, just let it rest, feeling the weight, temperature, and shape of it on your tongue. Then notice the taste as well.

When you've observed the physical sensations, notice also your thoughts and feelings and urges.

Slowly allow your tongue to move. Explore the changing textures and all the flavors, from the bitter to the sweet.

Listen to the sounds. Notice the smells and sensations. Be aware of any images or movies that float through your head—perhaps about the journey this food took, perhaps other times you've eaten something like this.

Become aware of your body's automatic responses, your stomach getting ready. Notice again thoughts and memories and feelings that may come up at the same time.

Now bite or chew the food and notice how it changes again.

You can continue to explore, even tuning in to each sense one at a time, feeling texture without taste, or noticing just sound.

And then, when you feel ready, swallow what's left of the food in your mouth.

Keeping your eyes closed, scan through your body, noticing what it feels like to be one piece of food bigger than you were a few moments ago in your body and in your mind.

When you ask a kid to wait until everyone has a portion before they begin, you can ask them to notice what the experience of waiting is like. You can also explore the experiences of surprise and curiosity by asking kids to close their eyes as you place the portion of food in their hand.

Follow-up questions can cover all aspects of the experience, from the sensory to the emotional. Depending on your kids, you can nudge the conversation toward dealing with urges, noticing thoughts and memories, or whatever feels relevant, while allowing the discussion to unfold organically. Usually I open with a joke like, "I don't know about you, but that's not the usual way I eat chocolate." But we can simply ask, "What did you notice?" "What surprised you?" "What *was* the experience—not *what did you think of the experience,* but what *was* it, with your senses and emotions?" "How did you know you liked it or disliked it?" "How did you know you were eating, what did your senses tell you?" "What happened before, during, and after eating?"

There is so much to be discovered in the simple act of eating when we pay close attention with our senses. Kids notice urges to speed up or slow down as they go; they notice color, texture, flavor, sounds, and all of the senses as they eat. And they become aware of their bodies preparing to eat and digest, which could lead into a lesson on biology. More than that, they may even notice the mind generating emotions, memories, associations, and thoughts triggered by the food. They may make connections to other people and even to ecology. Thich Nhat Hanh asks us to see if we can "taste the cloud" in our food and drink.

We typically think of eating something like a piece of chocolate as wonderful, but bear in mind that many people have more ambivalent feelings and associations about food. One girl I worked with actually started crying, feeling shame at the memory of having stolen her sister's Halloween candy the previous year. Many people have guilt around eating because of internalized voices from others shaming them about food or body image. We are there to help the children process the experience. However, for kids who may restrict their eating or have anorexia, I would not recommend this practice.

Always take allergies and food restrictions into consideration. If you are working with kids other than your own, it is wise to ask their parents or caregivers what they prefer their kids eat or not eat. Some foods kids may just not like, but we can invite kids to explore the experience with as many of their other senses as they feel comfortable with and then decide whether to taste the food. This may even lead to curiosity and a bite, and whether they end up liking the food or not, they can explore more deeply the experience of dislike. Don't forget to supply napkins and also possibly water.

THE BENEFITS OF MINDFUL EATING

Mindful eating has many benefits. We make contact with the present moment and build gratitude for our food. Often when we slow down, we enjoy the experience more, we eat less, and in turn, we make healthier food choices. Research shows that we get the signal from our body to stop eating about ten or even twenty minutes before that signal hits the brain.[8] When we slow down, we often eat less, eat more healthfully, and digest the food and nutrients better than when we rush or eat while doing something else. (Consider how much more you eat while in front of the TV or how that impossibly big bag of popcorn disappears halfway into the movie.) As lunchtimes at school get shorter and distractions abound, we eat faster and faster. I learned recently that high-schoolers in New York eat their lunches in an average of seven minutes! Slowing down and savoring in this way, especially with foods we love and appreciate, brings more joy to eating.

While eating an entire meal mindfully on a regular basis may be hard for those of us in the modern world, many of us do have time to have a "mindful meal Monday" or make an intention to take the first few bites of a meal or eat our dessert a little more slowly and mindfully, on any night or maybe just on certain holidays. We can even just put our cutlery down between bites, or chew each bite a certain number of times before swallowing. A therapist in a school I consult for does a lunch group with kids and finds it impossible to get them to not wolf down most of their food since they are so hungry. Her solution is to ask them to put aside three bites of their meal; at the end, they mindfully eat those last three bites together.

Or when we eat, we just eat—with no TV, radio, cell phones, tablets, books, or other distractions. We can intentionally appreciate where our food came from, maybe even getting involved in growing and making our own food. Mindful gardening, mindful cooking, and mindful food preparation all complement mindful eating.

∪

We live every day of our lives in our bodies, but often we seem to inhabit only our heads. With the exception of professional performers and athletes, most jobs that our culture values are rooted in the mind, not the body, which only reinforces the mind–body duality. But introducing mindful body-awareness practices to kids at younger ages creates a stronger foundation for health, happiness, learning, and compassion across the life span. Our bodies can become our allies, supporting us throughout our lives, if we learn to attend to and befriend them, to come into alignment and alliance with them.

CHAPTER 7

going with the flow

mindfulness and movement

I went out for a walk and finally concluded to stay out till
sundown, for going out, I found, was really going in.

JOHN MUIR, *John of the Mountains: The Unpublished Journals of John Muir*

⋃

Mindfulness does not happen only on meditation cushions. Many of
the best mindfulness practices for kids are done not in stillness, but
in movement. Focusing on a still body presents a challenge, which is
why contemplative movement practices, such as ritual dance, sport,
and martial arts, exist in so many cultures. We often think of yoga
and tai chi as practices that encourage mindful movement, but there
are dozens, if not hundreds, of other practices from around the world
that combine movement with meditative awareness. And we can bring
mindfulness to any movement we do in our daily lives. For active
kids especially, movement offers countless opportunities for practicing
mindful awareness.

Integrating mindfulness into movement has the added benefit
of combining mental exercise with physical exercise. Even a small
amount of physical exercise has powerful effects on wellness, physical
health, and even mental health.[1] Studies abound showing the benefits of simply walking for depression or anxiety, not to mention our

physical wellness. Yet even as we increase our understanding of the benefits of physical exercise, it is being cut out of formal and informal childhood curricula. Mindful movement helps our children develop and flourish physically, as well as emotionally and cognitively.

Walking is a movement we do every day, usually without much thought. This chapter is primarily devoted to walking meditations, in which we bring deliberate attention to the experience of walking in formal practice and in daily life.

Getting outside to walk in nature can also open kids' eyes, offering them new perspectives, different from those they encounter indoors or inside their electronics. Richard Louv, among others, writes about "nature-deficit disorder" and how it affects the physical and emotional health of our children.[2] Other studies found that just a little exposure to green spaces boosts happiness and attention. Many of us have experienced the power of nature to soothe our most challenging emotions. The natural world is full of lessons to be learned and metaphors to be explored.

Basic Walking Meditation

A basic walking meditation is pretty simple. All you need to do is notice yourself walking as you walk, making your body sensations the anchor of the meditation. To break out of walking on autopilot, perhaps you ask yourself, "How do I know I am walking?" and then check in with your senses. It also helps to bring awareness to certain aspects of walking. For example, you can bring mindfulness to your body as you notice the sensation of your feet on the ground or the movement of your muscles. Notice not just what your legs are doing, but also your arms, torso, spine, and head as you walk. You might be able to detect subtle shifts in your pulse, body temperature, or breathing rate before, during, and after walking. You can also focus on the gentle rocking motion of your weight shifting.

Though you don't have to walk slowly (or do the zombie walk, as kids inevitably joke), slowing down makes it easier to notice the subtleties of walking. But experimenting with different speeds is also fun.

Sometimes when we use our breath as our anchor meditation, we focus on the point between the in-breath and the out-breath, where there is a moment of stillness. Similarly, in walking, we can notice the points of stillness where the right step becomes the left step and the left step becomes the right step.

For adults and older kids, mindful walking has a tremendous amount to offer. Almost all of the kids I've worked with tell me that mindful walking is the practice they like and use more than any other, partly because it's so portable and so easy.

ADAPTING THE WALKING MEDITATION FOR KIDS

Just focusing on the body in motion can be hard for younger kids, with their shorter attention span and confusion about what the point of mindful walking is. Thich Nhat Hanh suggests having smaller kids take a few steps mindfully and then run around a bit before resuming mindful walking. One simple way to focus their attention is to have them count in rhythm with their steps. When they lose count, they can return to one again, making sure to do so with acceptance and nonjudgment. Below are many other ideas you can try.

WALKING WITH WORDS

It may help to have something to say along with the movements. The words can be abstract. We can, for example, say *thank you* and send gratitude or compassion to our feet and body as we move—a practice from Christopher Germer and Kristin Neff's program Mindful Self-Compassion. Or we can quietly or internally repeat reminder phrases to ourselves.

Younger kids may like saying the following four lines suggested by Thich Nhat Hanh, one line per step:

> I have arrived,
> I am home,
> in the here,
> in the now.

Teens and older kids may like some phrases I heard from Noah Levine, saying one with each step:

> Nowhere to go.
> Nothing to do.
> No one to be.

You and your kids can come up with your own phrases for walking, too.

WALKING WITH EMOTIONS

Bringing awareness of our emotional experience to walking adds another dimension to a walking meditation. For example, you can ask your kids to notice what it feels like for them to approach others or to be near others' personal space (see Personal Space Practice in chapter 6). Or you could ask them to smile at everyone they encounter, making their walking meditation a version of the Smile Meditation in chapter 9. In a larger group, a natural physical and emotional rhythm often starts to form as people move, which might be interesting to discuss.

Kids of all ages often describe how self-conscious they feel at first, deliberately walking around in a group, wondering if everyone else is paying as much attention to their walk as they are. Asking them what that experience of self-consciousness feels like in the mind and body, and how they cope with it, can be a rich discussion. Others might describe feeling micro emotions of excitement when walking into the sunshine, or dread when the smallest hill approaches, or curiosity about their surroundings.

You can explore other aspects of walking and being in a group simply by having the kids take turns leading and following and shifting the pace. Afterward, you can ask kids what it felt like to lead a group in walking and then what it was like to follow another person. These questions can open up conversations about trust, patience, and other rich topics.

WALK THIS WAY!

With younger kids, you can use visualization and imagination to make walking meditation a fun game that's easier to focus on. You could have them:

- walk like they are on slippery, thin ice over a lake

- walk like they are barefoot on hot sand or molten lava

- walk like they are balancing a bucket of ice water on their head

- walk like they are trying to be completely silent

- walk like they are in low gravity or extreme gravity

- keep their belly button perfectly level while walking

- walk like a penguin, a lion, or another favorite animal

- walk "as if you are kissing the earth with your feet," as Thich Nhat Hanh says

Use your imagination to create a story to engage the kids. Why are they trying to walk as quietly as possible? Are they a group of spies? What could be the destination or treasure they are trying to get to across the frozen lake?

You can also take a page from the theater games many of us did in high school and ask kids to walk as if they were experiencing a particular emotion or as a particular person, a practice Deborah Schoeberlein suggests in *Mindful Teaching and Teaching Mindfulness*. This activity encourages the development of compassion and empathy, the ability to get into the heads of other people. It also promotes insight into the ways body language communicates messages, both to themselves and to the world. You can give all the kids the same emotion, or you can assign different emotions to different kids. During the walk, periodically ring a bell or make another signal to have everyone stop, breathe, and shift into a different emotion.

WALKING CHARACTERS

You could have the kids pick their character out of a hat and then walk like that character. Characters in the hat could include:

- an angry bully

- a confident businesswoman

- a grieving widow

- a celebrity walking down the red carpet

- a model walking down the runway

- someone very shy

- a guy who just won the lottery

- a student who just failed a test

- a young person

- an old person

- an actor walking onstage to receive an Academy Award

- a five-year-old with ADHD

- the captain of the lacrosse team

- someone meeting an old friend they haven't seen in years

- a heartbroken middle-schooler

- yourself

I'm sure you can think of many more characters, and the kids can call them out too. You could also use animals, from timid mice to brave lions, and explore these as well. But before you begin, consider what emotions or archetypes might be triggering in ways that could overwhelm some kids. Also, consider what emotions and archetypes might be helpful for certain kids.

The practice of walking in the shoes of another person can lead to a rich conversation afterward. Ask them how the other personalities they walked in differ from their own walking and personality. Kids often notice that how they walked and acted affected how they felt about others and the environment around them. Some might point out that when they were the sad widow or shy child, they noticed little about the world around them because their eyes were downcast. Others might notice that by pretending to be confident, they actually felt confident. Exploring different characters and emotions can be truly eye-opening.

SILLY WALKING

One fun suggestion, from Jan Chozen Bays' book *How to Train a Wild Elephant,* is silly walking.[3] Perhaps some readers are old enough to remember the Monty Python comedy sketch about the Ministry of Silly Walks. (You can easily find it online by searching "Ministry of Silly Walks.") It's a hilarious sketch, and watching it can inspire both kids and adults to shake off some of their self-consciousness and walk in as silly a way as they can. Not only is silly walking fun, but staying balanced while doing so usually requires an incredible amount of attention. Silly walking is also a good activity for helping kids "get the sillies out" so they can then shift gear and transition into progressively less silly walks to calm themselves.

SENSORY AWARENESS WALKING

This adaptation for the walking meditation is simple. I learned it from meditation teacher Chas DiCapua on a mindfulness retreat for teens.

> First walk while keeping your eyes still and watching the view change.
>
> Then focus just on the soles of your feet, noticing different sensations.
>
> Then focus on sounds—your own, and the ones in the world as you move.
>
> Then focus on smells and tastes in the air.
>
> Then notice everything at once.

5-4-3-2-1 WALKING

A variation on Sensory Awareness Walking was taught to me by a workshop participant, Annie Nelson. She asks the kids to walk outside, and notice and describe:

5 Beautiful things they see

4 Sounds they hear

3 Sensations they feel

2 Things they smell or taste

1 Thought they are having

PENNY WALKING

Try having kids attempt to walk while balancing coins on their bare feet or shoes. This can be a hilarious endeavor, providing ample opportunity to discuss a range of reactions to the challenge. It especially offers lessons in what frustration feels like and how we respond to it. If walking with one coin gets too easy, add more coins. Both the distractions—the inevitable sounds of coins rolling and laughter that follows—and the group focus are contagious, which is another interesting point for discussion.

Similarly, old games like walking while carrying an egg on a spoon or a full glass of water can bring more awareness and attention to the simple act of walking.

APPRECIATIVE WALKING

Paying attention to our surroundings is another way to bring deliberate awareness to walking, and to change our perception of the world.

You might be familiar with the idea of positive psychology, which is often misunderstood. Positive psychology is not about pretending things are positive when they aren't or pretending you're happy about them when you're not. It's about recalibrating our built-in "negativity bias" so that we see the world in a balanced and realistic way. To survive, our ancestors needed to be on the lookout for danger and negative things in their environment. One bug of evolution is that we still tend to notice the negative—what's bad or potentially hazardous around us. It may be hard to believe, but modern life really is safer than our cave-dwelling and hunter-gatherer days. A saying in positive psychology is, "Our brains are Teflon for the positive and Velcro for the negative." Positive psychology is about changing that, so that positivity and negativity stick in our brains equally. If we come with a built-in filter for the negative, we can change that through appreciation and gratitude practices, which allow us to see things as they truly are.

When I explained positive psychology to Sophie, one of my clients, she reflected for a moment and summed it up as only a teenager could:

"Oh, I get it. Because I used to think if I paid attention to just the positive, I'd step in dog shit. But it's not that I'm pretending the dog shit isn't there. It's that I'm *also* noticing that the sunshine and everything else is there too."

My friend Christopher Germer points out that positive psychology practices such as gratitude and appreciation, which allow us to see the world more clearly, are truly practices that build wisdom.

One experiment asked a group of college students to take a twenty-minute walk a few times a week.[4] The participants were divided into three groups. One group was instructed to notice and contemplate the positive, focusing on the sunshine, flowers, and other positive things they encountered as they walked. The second group was to focus on the negative, the noise and pollution around them. The last group was just asked to take a walk.

The results after a week were about as expected: the positive group's overall mood improved, the negative group's overall mood was worse, and the control group felt a little better as a result of getting some exercise. The longer-term results held one surprise: months down the road, the positive group reported that they continued to feel more positive and happy.

These results are the inspiration for another walking practice: to simply notice the beauty in the world around us as we walk. It may be a tree beginning to blossom, a particularly beautiful shaft of light, a house or car painted a favorite color. If there is a walk you take with your kids regularly, you can make a regular practice of asking them to notice one positive thing—something beautiful, something funny, or perhaps an act of kindness—along the way. They can record these things in a journal or share them with others.

Eliza, a young woman I worked with, was anxious about school. Her long walk to high school each day was a movie trailer for the day's coming horrors until she practiced appreciative walking. As dreary winter settled on New England, she took it on herself to start photographing small pieces of color in the perpetual wintry gray on her walk—a red berry covered in melting ice, pine needles resting on the snow. She was able to soak up the good feelings that came with it. She posted her photos on a blog of mindful photography. If she were doing it now, it would probably be an Instagram hashtag.

Finding moments of positivity or beauty on a commute or on a walk to school can be particularly helpful, as research shows that commuting is often the most stressful part of the day for adults and kids alike. Appreciative walking (or commuting) can transform that stressful experience into an opportunity for mindfulness practice.

CAN WE ACT OUR WAY INTO A NEW WAY OF THINKING AND FEELING?

Changing how we hold and move our bodies dramatically changes how we feel. Business professors Amy Cuddy, Dana Carney, and Andy Yap studied how postures and poses affect how we feel and how we are perceived in the short and long run.[5] We know that body language communicates to others; they studied what body language communicates to ourselves. They found that certain "high-power poses" (think of Wonder Woman or Superman standing tall, with chest out and hands on hips) increase certain hormones in our bodies, which in turn creates higher confidence and lower stress. "Low-power poses" seem to do the opposite. A body shrunk in on itself—poor posture, shoulders in, arms closed, head down, hand on the back of the neck—led to an increase in stress hormones and a decrease in confidence-related hormones. When research subjects assumed a high-power pose for only two minutes just before a fake job interview, they landed the fake job more often, and they were described as having greater presence and personality than the other subjects.

Doing power poses with kids can be a great lesson. Mindfulness doesn't have to mean sitting still on a cushion; mindfully moving and changing our body posture—in yoga, power poses, or even in the stress-response exercise in chapter 1—can change how we see ourselves and the world around us, as well as how the world sees us.

Mindfulness in Sports and Fitness

A sport or fitness activity that emphasizes form and cultivates concentration is a natural opportunity to bring mindful attention to the body and its surroundings. This can be almost any sport, but particularly:

Archery	Crew/rowing
Dance	Fencing
Fly-fishing	Golf
Gymnastics	Hiking
Martial arts	Parkour
Rock climbing	Running
Sailing	Skating
Skiing	Surfing
Tennis	Yoga

Yoga is a concentration practice that prepares the body and mind for meditation, but can be made mindful as we notice where our minds wander off to as we practice. Balance poses offer great lessons in the power of a still mind. Try doing tree pose, or just standing on one leg, while distracted, emotional, laughing at a funny joke, or even with eyes wandering around the room; the body and balance inevitably collapse. Our bodies contain much wisdom, and different poses trigger different emotions, different memories, and different urges for different people. Just paying attention to what comes up as we practice poses, without judging, is a mindfulness practice in itself.

Our bodies can also be illustrations. Storytime yoga, a wonderful program I recently learned about, integrates yoga postures into stories kids write themselves, teaching both body awareness and written reflection. In "moving stillness," another practice, you try to move your entire body while keeping one part complete still, then allow the stillness of that part to slowly spread throughout your body, training the mind and body to focus.

Mindfulness in sports doesn't have to be just those sports that seem meditative. Competitive team sports like basketball, hockey, and soccer can also incorporate elements of mindfulness to help athletes improve their game, as many famous (and championship-winning) athletes have learned. Legend has it that coach Phil Jackson would have members of the Los Angeles Lakers mindfully put on their socks in the locker room before games. Many coaches use guided visualization with their teams to practice form, such as for shooting free throws, while others teach awareness practices to help players stay alert and follow the ball, or use breathing practices to help players tune in with their teammates and regulate their stress in the face of millions of fans.

CHAPTER 8

shortcut to the present

using sound and our senses

Between stimulus and response, there is a space.
In that space lies our freedom and our power
to choose our response. In our response
lies our growth and our happiness.

ANONYMOUS, often misattributed to Viktor Frankl[1]

∪

When our mind is untrained, our thoughts race to the future, to the past, anywhere but here. Unlike our mind and thoughts, our five senses are always in the present and thus available to ground us. At the same time, our senses can trigger a distraction or divergence: a sound turns into an image and a story, a smell brings up the emotions of another time, a sensation brings an instant judgment of like or dislike. From these reactions there is much to be learned—insights to be had about triggers, likes and dislikes, desires and aversions, and the patterned and conditioned ways we respond to them.

Our senses are what remind us we are alive, and they allow us to appreciate and savor everything that life offers. Helen Keller once asked a friend who had been out walking in the forest what she had seen on her walk. "Nothing in particular," the friend responded. Shocked at her friend's response, Keller was inspired to write an essay on what she would do if she had her sight back for three days. In it she wrote:

> I who am blind can give one hint to those who
> see—one admonition to those who would make use of
> the gift of sight: Use your eyes as if tomorrow you would
> be stricken blind. And the same method can be applied
> to the other senses. Hear the music of voices, the song
> of a bird, the mighty strains of an orchestra, as if you
> would be stricken deaf tomorrow. Touch each object
> as if tomorrow your tactile sense would fail. Smell the
> perfume of flowers, taste with relish each morsel, as if
> tomorrow you could never smell and taste again. Make
> the most of every sense; glory in all the facets of pleasure
> and beauty which the world reveals to you through the
> several means of contact which Nature provides.[2]

The passage delightfully demonstrates the power of mindfulness, the beauty of our senses, and the virtues of appreciation and gratitude. It also serves as a reminder that many people in this world don't have all of their senses as fully intact as yours may be.

This chapter could be infinitely long and delve into dozens of practices that engage any or all of the five senses. For the sake of brevity, it will focus on sounds and our sense of hearing, though I offer some suggestions for engaging other senses in our mindfulness.

Many people use bells, chimes, singing bowls, and such to mark the start or end of a meditation practice. If these feel too spiritual, you can also use tone bars, tuning forks, triangles, drums, musical instruments, and even rain sticks to mark transitional moments in a meditation.

DISAPPEARING SOUND

A simple, introductory listening practice for kids is to ask them to close their eyes and listen to the sound of a bell or chime that has a long reverberation. Ask them to listen carefully to the beginning, middle, and end of the sound, then raise their hand when the sound has completely disappeared for them.

This practice is a lovely way to signal the start and end of a practice, whether you're doing that practice at home, in a classroom, or elsewhere. I open and close many of my own meetings with patients, coworkers, or supervisees with the sound of a bell. Dueling Sounds is a variation: ring two bells at once, and ask kids to shift their awareness between the two sounds as each one lingers and passes.

SURFING THE SOUNDSCAPE

This sound meditation can be made longer or shorter by changing the number of cues you include. It might help to turn off any machines that make white noise or to crack a window or door. With novices, younger kids, or kids with short attention spans, try five or ten seconds (two to three breaths) between cues. For kids with longer attention spans, try twenty to thirty seconds.

Take a few minutes to settle in and explore the soundscape around you. With each sound that arrives, tune in to it and notice what the mind does. Perhaps it begins to show a movie or tell a story, triggers a thought or emotion, or recalls a memory. Notice this happening, and then just return to listening.

You might tune into sounds above you . . . or sounds below you.

Sounds to the left . . . and to the right.

Sounds behind you . . . and in front of you.

If the mind is carried off or wanders away with a sound, just gently return to listening.

Notice sounds that are near. Notice sounds that are far away.

Sounds outside the building. Sounds inside the building. Sounds inside the room.

Sounds of your own body—maybe even sounds like your thoughts, inside your own body.

From here, you might have the kids shift to noticing different kinds of sounds.

 Now let's explore the different types of sounds we're hearing.
Human sounds.
Nature sounds.
Machine sounds.
Notice what it's like to experience pleasant sounds and how the mind responds to them.
Notice what it's like to experience unpleasant sounds and how the mind responds to them.
Notice sounds that are constant. Sounds that are changing. Sounds that are regular and steady. And sounds that are random.
If the mind wanders away to follow a particular sound, just return to listening.

You can continue the meditation by exploring the different responses our minds and bodies have to different sounds, including how we sense sounds with other parts of our body, beyond our ears.

Now try leaning in to hear sounds.
And try leaning back, to let sounds land on you.
Try tuning in to just one sound and really listening in, exploring its features to see if it has a shape, a texture, a color, or an emotion.
Try zooming back out and holding in your ears all of the sounds at once. Can you experience them all simultaneously?
Try listening with your whole body. As each sound comes, feel the vibrations where the sound lands in your body. Let each sound land softly, like rain.

See if you can experience the sound just as the sound, before your ears and brain make a story or meaning out of it.

Then return to just listening, just receiving.

Now return to noticing the sound, watching what the mind does, and gently leading it back to listening, again and again—just seeing what the mind does.

And as we come to the end of this practice, remember you can come back to the present at any moment by dropping into the soundscape for just a moment or just a few sounds.

Sounding a bell is an appropriate way to end this meditation. Before you do, say, "As I ring the bell, follow the sound of the bell fading out as you tune in to your other senses. When you can no longer hear it, open your eyes, wiggle your toes, and bring all of your senses back into the room."

I love to introduce this meditation in places like schools, because kids and staff alike are often skeptical about practicing mindfulness in such a loud and chaotic setting. This meditation turns the object of distraction, sound, into the anchor for our attention. In the process, it transforms our relationship to the distraction and helps us see first-hand that *what we resist persists*.

This meditation holds deeper lessons, such as how to transform other frustrations into objects of attention. For example, paying attention to unpleasant sounds can offer insight into physical or emotional discomfort, how to listen to feelings of depression or anxiety, or how to understand what the mind does with unpleasant or frustrating experiences. Exploring our response to an annoying sound offers the opportunity to also explore how we respond to an annoying emotion or an annoying person. Starting with just one simple sound, we learn how thought ripples outward and how insight can be gained from paying attention to everything, even the inevitable unpleasant things in our lives.

This meditation can lead to conversations about emotional triggers. The sound of a ticking clock, for example, stresses out clients worried about time or deadlines. We are taking in thousands of sounds on a daily basis, and these sounds are always triggering us, below the level of conscious awareness. When we do this practice deliberately and carefully, we help children learn to deal with whatever arises from their triggers, holding the space so they can work through them.

As a therapist, I used this practice myself when I noticed my anxiety increasing during a family therapy session. I realized I was hearing the sound of a father anxiously picking at the foam of his coffee cup, and that sound was making his anxiety spread to the rest of us. So, this practice can help us settle and get a sense of the emotions in a room or in a group.

You can make this practice into a game by asking kids to listen and, in the silence, write down (or draw) as many sounds as they can. You can ask them to note differences in sounds that at first might seem to be the same—different bird chirps, different trees in the wind, and so on. One musical teen I work with took inspiration from this practice to go "soundhunting" and record "found sounds" in the city to use as samples in music he creates.

Surfing the Soundscape as Daily Informal Practice

Listening can be formal, as above, or informal. We all know to count to ten to calm down, but the practice of counting to five or ten *sounds* is more effective, interesting, and containing. Some of my more anxious kids do this silently to focus themselves before a test, a performance, or an athletic competition.

A few years back I worked with a survivor of a bombing attack who found himself constantly on edge, his brain having been reset by the trauma. By deliberately making himself vigilant and grounding himself in the reality of the present, rather than his fears of it, he was able to regain control and calm himself in situations where he would have panicked. His favorite two practices were counting to five sounds and counting to five sensations in his body when he walked into new rooms and situations. Counting body sensations reminds us that our four other senses are also available to us and can be used in similar ways.

In another informal variation of this meditation, we share sounds back and forth with another person. With kids, we might count to ten sounds together with them, taking alternating turns naming what we hear and what each sound makes us think of.

Music and Mindfulness

Many kids love their music, iPods, and headphones. Listening to music can be an effective way to cope with stress. In my work, I spend time helping kids brainstorm coping skills they can use in difficult moments, and listening to music often ends up toward the top of the list. When kids ask me how they can listen to music mindfully, I offer the following practices.

ONE-TRACK MINDFULNESS PRACTICE

Sometimes favorite songs lose their freshness and emotional impact. This practice makes our old favorites sound new again.

 Put on headphones or crank up the volume of your speakers and do *nothing but listen* to a favorite song. See if you can tune into just one instrument or sample track that runs through the song. Many songs now have dozens of tracks layered onto one another, and by listening in this deliberate way, it becomes possible to notice new, previously unheard aspects of a song, making it fresh again.

LET THE MUSIC MOVE YOU (EMOTIONALLY)

For kids who struggle with identifying their emotions before those emotions take over, I suggest the following practice.

Pick three songs: a favorite happy song, a sad song, and an angry song.

> Lie down, close your eyes, turn up the volume, and *just listen* to each song. As you listen, notice where in your body you feel the emotion arising, and notice what the emotion really feels like in your body.

This practice of listening mindfully and with the whole body offers a lesson in emotional intelligence, or emotional fluency—the ability to recognize and work with emotions as they arise in real time. Frustrating, confused, or fearful songs would be interesting to use in this practice, but they are harder to find in pop music. A film student once pointed out to me that movie or TV soundtracks often include music to trigger a broad range of emotions, including anxiety and uncertainty (think of the famous soundtracks to *Jaws* or *Psycho*). Mindfully listening to music and noticing how our emotions change with different songs can also help kids calm themselves down and shift their emotions. For example, they can make a playlist that starts with a silly song and gradually downshifts toward slower, calmer songs.

MORE THAN WORDS

This practice invites kids to notice how they respond to meaningful words. I saw researcher Willoughby Britton do something like this in a presentation. Here is the beginning of a practice script:

> Sit quietly with eyes closed or downcast. I'm going to say a few words. You just notice how your body responds to these words, or how your mind makes movies or tells stories when you hear them. Notice the ripples of thought that happen as I drop just these word pebbles into the pond of our still mind.

From there, speak a single word aloud, pause a moment, and ask the kids to notice their first reaction to the word—perhaps an emotion, an image, or a thought. You can invite them to share that reaction immediately, or ask them to write it down to share in discussion after the practice.

Some interesting words to drop in (or not, depending on your kids):

birthday	holiday
party	deadline
middle school	homework
bully	work
trouble	anniversary
dating	teenager

Adults may have different responses to a word than a kid has, and kids of different ages or in different moods will have different responses. Comparing the differences in people's reactions makes for an interesting discussion afterward.

∪

Our perceptual senses are the most direct pathway to the present moment, and paying attention to them is a way to watch the mind's reactions and thus come to understand the mind better. We can discover and intensify our senses by tuning various senses in or out, such as with games in which we wear blindfolds as we smell or feel various objects. Creativity and willingness are all you need to create your own sense practices.

CHAPTER 9

playing attention

games, play, and creative mindfulness

You can discover more about a person in an hour
of play than in a year of conversation.

Widely attributed to PLATO

U

For kids, play is a vital part of mental, social, and emotional development. We have the Internet for information and computers for some calculations, but in the future we will need people who can creatively solve problems, think critically, and lead with compassion. Play teaches kids all these skills, and so much more. It builds fine and gross motor skills as well as social skills, by encouraging cooperation, compromise, and compassion. Both free play and structured play cultivate perspective, build patience, and develop emotional intelligence. In therapy, play helps children, both verbal and nonverbal, process difficult relationships and experiences rather than act out because of them. Watching our children at play tells us much about how they perceive and interact with their world.

The structured play of games has long been a regular part of childhood. Childhood games reflect the values we teach our children and how we prepare them for the world. I noticed a number of years ago that kids from different backgrounds play different games, or they play the same games but with different rules. The differences prepared them for the different worlds they would grow into. In the inner city, both the card game Uno and the sport of basketball were played with high stakes and unpredictable, winner-take-all rules; it was also harder to get into a game and know where you stood when playing than when you were playing the same game in the suburbs, where the rules were consistent and clear. The differences starkly mirrored the kids' worlds and their futures. I noted that cooperation was emphasized in certain groups and competition was emphasized in others.

When I was growing up, we played games, in and out of school, that reinforced values like careful listening, impulse control, and executive functioning. And no, they weren't special games at all. Just think back to Freeze Tag, Simon Says, and Mother May I; these and similar games are actually lessons and practice. Other games, such as I Spy or Twenty Questions, teach inductive reasoning. Consider for a moment: What do today's games teach kids? And are kids able to learn the lessons these games teach when they have smaller amounts of free time in which to play them?

The games our kids play—video games, physical games, board and card games—are practice for real life. They are where kids begin to internalize values they will carry into adulthood. When we bring mindfulness and compassion into games, we teach kids mindfulness and compassion. Whether they realize it or not, we have planted the seeds that will enable them to grow into mindful and compassionate adults.

Adapting Existing Games to Bring in Mindfulness

With simple adaptations, many games can incorporate elements of mindfulness. For example, a colleague of mine adapted Candyland to teach emotional awareness. (Anything that makes Candyland more interesting is a good thing, because, as far as I'm concerned, it was created to torture adults with boredom.) She created a set of rules in which red cards were equated with anger. When a kid drew a red card, they were invited to describe a time they were mad, or what anger feels like, or what makes them mad, or what they can do when they are mad to deal with the emotion. Likewise, blue cards denoted sadness, and yellow cards happiness. The colors matter less than the general idea. I've used the same adapted rules and added that orange cards ask you to take one mindful breath, purple cards ask you to notice one sensation in your body, and green cards ask you to notice one sound.

Some therapists write questions on the sides of Jenga blocks, and invite kids to answer the question when the block is removed. Breathing and mindfulness practices could just as easily be written on the blocks. Practices can be written on the backs of cards, for games like Concentration and Memory. A bingo card could be made with twenty-four short practices on it. Checkers could have color-coded stickers that denote a short practice to be done when a piece is captured.

A game might start with a mindful breathing practice, such as the 7–11 Breath or Soup Breathing (chapter 11). Pausing to take a mindful breath before rolling the dice or taking a turn works with children of any age. We can slow down and talk through all possibilities for a move in a game, revealing the many choices we have at any moment. Doubtless you and your creative child collaborators will think of countless more adaptations for games that already exist.

Mindfulness Games

We can make existing games mindful, and we can also make mindfulness practice into something of a game. Here are two examples.

DR. DISTRACTO

My colleague and friend Mitch Abblett has kids practice mindfulness at the therapeutic school he directs. He uses this mindfulness game with groups of six- to eleven-year-old kids. All the kids practice a mindfulness task, while one gets to be Dr. Distracto. The doctor's job is to do a silly (but appropriate) behavior to distract the group from their mindfulness practice. The last kid to move or smile at the distraction gets to be Dr. Distracto for the next round.

FIND THE SONG

Author Deborah Plummer offers a game in which she hides a ticking clock or wireless speaker and asks kids to find it based on where the sound is coming from. Kids can close their eyes, listen carefully, and then point in the direction the song is coming from.

SMILE MEDITATION

There's a saying, usually attributed to Thich Nhat Hanh, that goes, "Sometimes your joy is the source of your smile, but sometimes your smile can be the source of your joy." This practice, which I learned from my friend Janet Surrey, works best when kids are seated in a circle, or at least not in rows.

Close your eyes or just relax them and let them rest on the floor in front of you.

Invite a smile to your lips. Notice what the sensations of the smile feel like. Also notice what your emotions are when you smile.

Now continue to smile while you open or raise your eyes and simply look around the room. Share a smile and eye contact with anyone you see, noticing what emotions come up as you do.

Once you've smiled at everyone in the room, lower your eyes, and take a moment to smile to yourself.

(Allow twenty seconds or more, depending on the size of the group, then ring the bell to signal the end of the session and open a discussion.)

You can have kids do this practice while walking around a small space. In this adaptation, omit the direction to have them close their eyes.

Another variation is to have the group send smiles to one person at a time in a "smile wave," as the smiles move around a circle.

If there are only two of you, you can just smile at each other for a few breaths, then lower your eyes again.

PASS THE BREATH

A great prop for sharing mindful breathing with young kids is a Hoberman sphere—an expanding ball toy. This practice, from my friend Fiona Jensen, incorporates a Hoberman sphere as a visual and kinetic aid. In general, this practice works best with the group positioned in a circle, sitting or standing.

You, the adult, will be the starting person. Hold the sphere in your hands, in its smallest, most compact position. Expand the sphere at the pace of your slow and mindful in-breath, and on the exhale contract the sphere again. Have everyone in the group breathe along with you. Then pass the sphere to the next person in the group and repeat.

With a group of six kids, you will have opened the ball with six mindful breaths (seven, if you participated too); in a classroom of twenty, with twenty mindful breaths. The practice cultivates group cohesion, as everyone aligns their breath. If it's just two of you, or you can pair up, you can pass the breath back and forth every three breaths until you get to a certain number or for a specific amount of time.

If you don't have a Hoberman sphere, various gestures or sounds can represent the breath as it is passed from one child to the next. The first person might say, "Breathing in," and then turn to the next person. Both, together, say, "Breathing out." Then the second person says, "Breathing in," and the pattern repeats.

THE HUMAN MIRROR

Another fun game for all ages that teaches paying attention to and attuning with others is the Human Mirror. Many of us played versions of this game when we were kids, and in retrospect we can see how much it cultivates interpersonal mindfulness.

You can do this practice as a partner with your child. The two of you should sit or stand facing each other. Decide which of you will be the leader first.

The leader begins by moving parts of his or her body, starting slowly and then speeding up. The other person mirrors the movement. After a minute or two, ring a bell or signal in another way that it's time to switch roles. Now your child moves, and you follow.

Continue taking turns for as long as you like.

In a variation, the leader makes different facial expressions representing different emotions. Another, more intense variation is to have the partners maintain eye contact the entire time and use only their peripheral vision to notice movement.

If you are doing this practice with two kids, you can take turns being the leader while the other two players follow. Or you, the adult, can be the facilitator and timekeeper while the kids play as a pair.

If you are doing this practice with a group, divide it into pairs. It's best to pair up the kids yourself, rather than deal with the anxieties of letting the kids choose partners. Before you begin, decide whether or not you want to include physical contact and, if so, how. You may want a musical accompaniment to inspire movement.

Large-Group Version: The Human Kaleidoscope (or the Human Mandala)

My therapist friend Ashley Sitkin taught me this version of the Human Mirror, which is suitable for more advanced groups. Create a circle with an even number of people and assign them partners directly across from each other within the circle. One partner takes the lead, making free movements with hands and arms, moving in and out as the other partner follows. Everyone else is doing the same, so that if the circle were viewed from above, there is some symmetry to it, as there is in a kaleidoscope. At the change signal, the players move on around in the circle, eventually coming back to their original positions. Another group variation is to have everyone mirror one person, who leads the entire group with their movements.

Cultivating Mindfulness Through Creativity

Play, games, and movement are ways to creatively engage kids in mindfulness. Arts, artistic expression, and creativity are other ways. Engaging in the arts teaches wonderful coping skills, and we can enhance that by bringing more mindfulness to the activity.

MINDFUL COLORING

I've been surprised at how powerful and calming the simple act of coloring, especially coloring certain types of patterns, can be when I'm working with clients of all ages. Forms like fractals, mandalas, Celtic knots, and labyrinth shapes all echo forms found in nature, and research suggests we are evolutionarily wired to feel calm and safe in the presence of such patterns. Carl Jung believed that mandala shapes tapped into the collective unconscious that is built into us as human beings. Similar patterns and archetypes are found across cultures.

One of my tougher kids, a few years back, was an eighteen-year-old who had just been released from jail. In one of our first meetings, I laid out some colored pencils and photocopies of fractal patterns, and soon enough he was carefully selecting pencils and coloring the patterns. Before he realized it, he had opened up and was talking about deep vulnerabilities, from his troubled relationship with his father to other intimate subjects that I never expected him to share. The power of these patterns is startling.

There are plenty of free images online and inexpensive coloring books available, including the trendy new genre of coloring books for adults. Fractals and mandalas are great abstract images for all ages. Many coloring books on mandalas have imagery that relates to different cultural heritages and that may be appealing to a diverse range of kids. Coloring books of art, architecture, and design motifs may also engage kids with different interests. Consider also the coloring tools—markers, crayons, or colored pencils—and how they encourage awareness of smell, sound, and touch, in addition to the visual act of coloring.

CLEARING THE CLOUDS

This creativity practice is another opportunity for creative expression. It is inspired by my colleague Joan Klagsbrun, an expert in focusing practice, which shares many commonalities with mindfulness. She has adapted the first step in the focusing process, called "clearing a space," for kids. All you need are some small pieces of paper, markers or crayons, and a small gift box or gift bag for each kid you're working with.

Place the drawing materials in front of each child, and place each child's bag or box in front of them a bit further away. Then follow this script:

> Take a moment and find your mindful posture, closing your eyes if you feel comfortable.
>
> Take three mindful breaths and tune in to feelings and emotions in your body. You can close your eyes if you like, and even put a hand over your heart to help you focus.
>
> Now, check in and see if there are any feelings or thoughts in the way of your happiness. If your heart is like the sun, are there any feelings that are like clouds blocking the sun's rays? Maybe a strong feeling?
>
> *(After allowing ten or twenty seconds for reflection, ring a bell or somehow signal a pause.)*
>
> Open your eyes and take a minute to write some words or draw a picture of what kind of cloud is blocking your inner sunshine.
>
> *(Give the kids about a minute to draw or write.)*
>
> Now, fold up your paper and place it in the box [or bag] in front of you.
>
> Take a few more breaths and tune in again. Is there anything else in the way of you being fully happy and present, of letting the sun shine?
>
> *(Give the kids another ten to twenty seconds, or until you see a lot of squirming and peeking.)*
>
> Once again, open your eyes and draw, doodle, or write down what that is, and put the paper in the box.

(Give the kids about a minute to draw or write.)

Take a few more breaths and tune in again. Is there anything else in the way of you being fully happy and present, of letting the sun shine?

(Give the kids another ten to twenty seconds.)

Once again, draw, doodle, or write it down and put it in the box.

(Give the kids about a minute to draw or write.)

Now, I'd like you to take the box and place it at whatever distance feels comfortable for now.

(Kids might set it a few feet in front of them; some may even get up and walk across the room to set down the box.)

Now, tune in and feel your inner sun shining. With each breath, let the clouds drift away and the sunshine appear. Now that you've cleared some space in front of the sun, for the rest of the day it may be easier to come back to your inner sunshine.

And now, take a few moments and see if any words or images come to mind about your inner sunshine, and draw or write about these on your last sheet of paper.

(Give the kids about a minute.)

We will finish for now. For the rest of the day, remember that you can always just take a few breaths, clear away the clouds, and tune in to your inner sunshine.

(Ring a bell or signal the end of the practice in another way.)

You can do many variations on this creative practice. Because I use little owl-shaped gift boxes I found at a party store, I say, "Give them [the drawings or words on the paper] to the wise old owl."

Other images and questions can be used to clear a path to the present moment or to happiness. You could have kids visualize a path in the woods and see the things that are blocking the path. You could ask them to imagine weeding a garden to let the beautiful flowers bloom, asking them what is in the garden that they don't want, and having them pull it out like a weed, or asking what is not in the garden that they do want, and having them plant it and give it water or sunshine. Younger kids will understand things in the way of their happiness; older or more experienced kids may appreciate clearing the clouds or a path to the present moment. You can also ask questions like, "Is there anything from the past or future in the way of the present?" Teens may not even need the drawings to identify these past and future elements.

Note: you will want to be sure the kids keep their boxes and that they don't end up in the wrong hands, or have everyone recycle their boxes together so that the kids feel safe.

WRITE YOUR OWN MINDFUL BREATHING MEDITATION

I first began my own mindfulness practice in earnest after a powerful retreat experience with Zen master Thich Nhat Hanh when I was taking time off from college. I bought his book *Being Peace*, which contains a series of wonderful images and words for breath meditations.[1] In that book he brings visualization and rhythm to the breath, which can be hard to focus on alone. These examples generally capture the idea:

Breathing in, I know that I am breathing in . . .
Breathing out, I know that I am breathing out . . .
In . . .
Out . . .

Breathing in, my breath grows deep . . .
Breathing out, my breath goes slowly . . .
Deep . . .
Slow . . .

Breathing in, I feel calm . . .
Breathing out, I feel ease . . .

Calm . . .

Ease . . .

Breathing in, I see myself as a flower . . .

Breathing out, I feel fresh...

Flower . . .

Fresh . . .

I have found using Thich Nhat Hanh's phrases and imagery particularly powerful with children. In his book *Planting Seeds*, he includes ways to make artistic activities out of these practices through drawing.[2]

These stanzas made up my earliest practice—the images and rhythms making it easy for my mind to stay focused and still as I practiced. I used a tape recorder (yes, it was that long ago) to record myself so I could listen later, and I soon realized the imagery was infinitely adaptable. Since that time, I've created new imagery in collaboration with kids and adults for their own meditations.

Consider your kids and what imagery might be helpful to them, given their background or what they are struggling with. Start with an image, perhaps of something natural, and then draw that image and contemplate its qualities. For example, for kids struggling with anxiety or impulsivity, still water might be a good image. Still water reflects the world around it clearly. Still water settles and has depth. Still water is calm, serene, and resting. When water is still, the reflections on it are not distorted, and even if there are ripples on its surface, it can be calm underneath, as experienced in the extended Stone in the Lake visualization practice in chapter 5.

Breathing in, I see myself as a lake.
Breathing out, I feel still and calm.
Lake . . .
Stillness . . .
(Repeat.)

Thich Nhat Hanh often begins with lines such as, "Breathing in, I know I am breathing in" or "My breath grows deep/slow," and then adds lines with imagery.

The formula is pretty simple: contemplate an object with the breath, then contemplate its healing qualities. Creating your own mindfulness meditation becomes almost like a *Mad Libs* game, incorporating imagery and the qualities that we are seeking to cultivate. Here are some prompts to help kids find imagery that works for them:

"Breathing in, I see myself as . . ." (an image: certain animals, trees, mountains, lakes, oceans, rivers, water, air, valleys, fire, flowers, sunshine, stars, earth, sky)

"Breathing out, I feel . . ." (qualities: strength, fearlessness, calm, bravery, reflection, stability, awareness, confidence, openness, perseverance, presence, generosity, flexibility, acceptance, courage, energy)

You can try variations using actions, such as "smile to myself," "accept myself," "am aware," "savor the moment," and "enjoy my breath," and then active words such as *watching, feeling, calming, caring, releasing, healing*. For example:

Breathing in, I smile to myself.
Breathing out, I accept myself as I am.
Smiling . . .
Accepting . . .

Another variation is to breathe in a desired quality and breathe out an undesired quality, such as stress, fear, or depression:

Breathing in, I breathe in relief.
Breathing out, I breathe out stress.
Relief . . .
Stress . . .

The variations are infinite. For a frightened child, you could pick a lion for bravery or a mountain for confidence: "Breathing in, I am a lion. Breathing out, I feel brave" or "Breathing in, I am a mountain. Breathing out, I am strong and confident." For a depressed child, try sunshine or sky: "Breathing in, I am the shining sun. Breathing out, I am the open sky."

The main idea is to have fun and write something together. You can then have the kids draw their images on a small piece of paper, mindfully bringing attention to the sights, sounds, and smells of drawing, and write their verses on the other side. They can share their drawings and verses with one another, if you're working with a group. You and they can also record their verses on their computers or smartphones so they can carry the words with them to listen to any time.

OTHER WRITING IDEAS

There are plenty of other writing activities that emphasize and teach both mindfulness and compassion. Recent research has shown that writing (and reading) first-person accounts increases compassion and empathy. Journaling and expressive writing have long been shown to benefit health and mental health.

∪

Play and creative expression are where new ideas and insights are born. On top of that, they are just plain fun. Regardless of how long it's been since you've played freely, played games, or practiced creativity, get out there (or get in there) and spend some time just playing. Find some toys, browse the aisles of a toy shop, sneak into your toy chest when the kids are gone, and let yourself explore. Smelling crayons, wetting your fingers with paint, making up goofy mindful lyrics to an existing song—whatever you choose to do, allow yourself to let go, step out of the judging mind, and just be in the moment. See what mindful games and practices arise out of letting yourself play or create freely, without adult self-consciousness, allowing new ideas and connections to arise. (And if you come up with anything good, let me know.)

THE BRAIN ON CREATIVITY

There are good reasons to use metaphor, poetry, and art
when we teach abstract concepts such as mindfulness, and
good reasons they are a big part of the mindfulness tradition.
Recent fMRI studies have looked at how the brain reacts to
hearing poetry, music, and other creative means of expression.

Hearing both poetry and music stimulated regions of the
brain associated with memory and emotion, and poetry also
lit up the posterior cingulate cortex and the medial temporal
lobes, both of which are associated with introspection.[3] So
maybe poets are deep after all.

We know that metaphors tap into something deep and
healing in the human unconscious (see chapter 5). A recent
study found that sensory parts of the brain light up in response
to sensory metaphors.[4] Engagement with the arts has also been
linked to better critical thinking and social tolerance.[5]

making the virtual virtuous

mindfulness and technology

> Once men turned their thinking over to machines in the hope that this would set them free. But that only permitted other men with machines to enslave them.
>
> FRANK HERBERT, *Dune*

⌣

I was flying to a conference to speak about mindfulness with young people last spring when I looked down to my tray table. My Macbook formed the base of a neat pyramid of trendy technologies, with my iPad on top of the laptop, and my iPhone resting on the iPad. It took a moment before I realized the absurdity of the scene in front of me: *I'm off to talk about the importance of staying in the moment and have no less than three gleaming Apple products sitting in front of me just to get through one cross-country flight?* I was grateful to be able to see the humor, but my next impulse was to take a picture and share the irony of it with friends online!

There's nothing inherently bad or good about technology. Technology just *is*. What we do with it and how we relate to it are what matters. A Zen adage says, "The thinking mind can be our most powerful servant or our most terrible master." It's an apt observation about the horrors our mind can create, but I often think of it in terms of the technology that surrounds us. It can seem like our communication devices are more often used to disconnect than to connect. Technology has made it easier to connect to information and to other people than at any time in human history. Our devices connect us more quickly, but not necessarily more deeply. And they disconnect us from ourselves as we become servants to them, rather than the other way around.

Technology has eased our lives in many ways, but it insulates us from human interaction. Instead of smiling at the checkout clerk (when we aren't shopping online or in the self-checkout lane), we stare into our phone while music pumps into our ears. Instead of asking directions from a passing stranger, we check our smartphone. When was the last time you walked into a meeting room and everyone was chatting rather than looking down their nose into their phone?

Linda Stone, the technology writer who invented the phrase "continuous partial attention" to describe the current state of our minds, has turned her research to email apnea—the phenomenon of our breathing becoming more stilted and shallow when we interact with our devices.[1] The way the breath changes when we are using technology is another example of how the breath can give us insight into our mental state. Texting and driving is a recognized public health issue, but even walking and texting is a serious issue. Multiple university students in my area have been struck by cars while crossing the street with phone in hand.

Using technology is addictive, in a very literal sense. Our use of technology is stimulated on what is called in behavioral studies a "variable rate reinforcement schedule." The term essentially means that our phone's random buzzing throughout the day acts as a little reward for the brain, which is rewired to crave more. This explains why we see kids (or catch ourselves) mindlessly refreshing email and social media feeds. Video games, slot machines, and phones are often designed by psychologists to maximize their addictive qualities.

Philosopher Alan Watts said that the great lie of television is that it tells us there is something more interesting happening somewhere other than the here and now. The Internet has supplanted television, and while it can get us the now faster than ever, it certainly takes us out of the here. Our devices hold out the false promise that there is something more important, more urgent, more interesting than our present-moment experience. Granted, this statement is not going to hold much water with a nine-year-old clutching an iPad, but I think you get the idea.

We can tell kids that they need healthy boundaries around screen time, or we can show them with our own actions, which is far harder but far more effective. I'm as guilty as anyone else; I love my gadgets and my social media. Ask yourself, how long do you spend in the morning checking in with yourself and your loved ones in person before you tap the glowing screen of your iPhone? Where is your phone right now? How do you feel when you don't know where it is? Do you usually keep it in your pocket, your bag, your desk, another room?

THE SEVENTY-NINTH ORGAN

At the 2013 Wisdom 2.0 conference, a presenter from Google gave a simple demonstration. I've adapted it into the following practice, called the Seventy-Ninth Organ. Try it with your kids, but also try it with your adult friends and colleagues.

The human body has seventy-eight organs. We need each of them to do its job to keep us alive and keep our physical system at equilibrium. If one were removed, we'd feel a sharp pain, and quickly our biological systems would be thrown out of balance.

These days, most of us also have a seventy-ninth organ, an external organ known as the smartphone. This is a good practice to use after a day without technology or to mark the end of a retreat period.

 Take out your phone now, if you don't have it in your hand already. Don't turn it on. Just notice how it feels in your hand. Notice your emotions, your urges, your body's response as you hold it—its familiar size, shape, and weight, suited to your hands.

Now find a partner near you. Turn on your phone and mindfully notice how you feel as the screen lights up.

Hand your phone to your partner.

How did it feel when you were asked to hand your phone to someone else? How did it feel to actually hand it to them? How do you feel when they are holding your phone?

After a moment, switch back.

Take a moment and reflect with your partner on this practice. What happened for you, and why do you think it did?

If you are doing this practice with a group, the pairs can come back to the larger group for a short discussion period.

Checking In and Checking Out

Don't like how you feel in the present moment? (And you shouldn't, if you believe most advertisements.) Are you even slightly bored? Check out something outside of yourself: watch a video, play a game, check your social media feeds. When we teach children to disconnect from their experience with digital distractions, it is no wonder they never learn basic emotional fluency and social cues, that emotions and urges arise and pass, and that human beings actually can tolerate discomfort. Even when we are happy, we are quick to remove ourselves from that experience and post a selfie of it. Kids and teens today have never lived without technology of instant distraction and instant gratification.

In our distracted world, the default setting is to check out. I was recently traveling through a small village in Burma, gazing around the dusty bus stop, drinking in the scene. Something felt different. It took me a moment, but then I realized that the passengers were looking up at the world around them, not down into their cell phones. How often in a moment of boredom do we automatically grab our device and see what is happening anywhere else in the world but where we are? Technology is only one distraction from how we feel in the present moment. Some people also turn to drugs, cutting, or other forms of acting out. We all have a host of distractions if we don't like how we feel inside. With all the distractions at your fingertips, you never need to be present with yourself or even experience true solitude.

Many of us see the consequences of this loneliness firsthand—not just in the record rates of mental illness among children, but in the young adults who simply never developed the capacity to be with themselves and their experience, let alone interact with others without technological mediation. Many young adults I encounter become overwhelmed when they finally have the independence to figure out who they are and what they want, and make their own life decisions.

Explicitly and implicitly, the way we live and the media we consume are teaching all of us to be lonely, to be too busy to attend to our needs, and to deal with emotions through looking outside of ourselves, rather than looking inside at the first twinge of discomfort.

Running counter to all of the checking out, mindfulness teaches us how to be with ourselves, a capacity for being alone. Mindful curiosity reveals that the present moment is both important and interesting. Checking in with the pleasant, the unpleasant, and the neutral aspects of our experience and the world around us is profoundly worthwhile. With mindfulness, we look inward, get in touch with the internal experience, tolerate it, and maybe even learn from it. In this way, we become happier and healthier.

Mindfulness teaches us not only how to be alone, but how to be in authentic connection with others as well. A friend I met on retreat a few years back runs the information technology department at a prestigious boarding school. He described a weekend storm that knocked the power out, leaving the campus offline for a few days. With "nothing to do," the students found fun and connection in other ways. Years later, many students recalled it as one of their favorite times at the school, and it was his as well (and he's the IT guy).

We can be intentional about taking time off from technology, and though we may face resistance at first, appreciation may ultimately set in. One family I work with turns off the wireless router for much of the day, and if the kids want the Internet, they plug in the old-fashioned way, with a cable. Since there is only one room where the cable can be connected, this rule at least keeps family members in the same room, and it makes connecting to the Internet an intentional act, not something done merely due to boredom. Other families and institutions have set hours when the Internet is on or off, or they have virtual quiet rooms where the router blocks access to some sites. Others set specific days or hours to be "technology sabbaths" or "phone-free Fridays," when we can truly be present for ourselves and those around us. Time away from technology has been shown to have significant benefits to social skills, as well as reducing stress.[2] Kids often worry about FOMO, the fear of missing out, but increasingly talk about the relief of unplugging and JOMO—the joy of missing out.

IDEAS FOR SETTING LIMITS AROUND TECHNOLOGY USE

- Establish tech-free times, such as the hour before bed or the first hour after waking up.

- Designate tech-free places, such as the dinner table, the car, the family room, or staff meetings.

- Try leaving your phone in the car or in your bag, rather than your pocket, while you run errands.

- Establish wireless hours and wired hours within the home.

- Lobby for virtual quiet rooms, where chat functions or social media are blocked, within schools, libraries, and other public venues.

- Only check messages when you can actually respond to them.

- Deliberately interact with people: ask someone for directions, chat with the shop clerk, and say hello to someone next to you rather than immediately looking into your phone.

Using, Not Abusing, Technology

We adults may wring our hands about the dangers of technology, and those dangers are very real. But the reality is that technology is not going anywhere, and we are often just as addicted as kids are. Our society has learned to maximize distraction and maximize the economic benefits of technology, but has not yet maximized technology's potential for health and happiness. This is the era in which we live, and most young people have no experience of the world without these devices. Rather than resisting, judging, and wringing our hands about the dangers of the wired world, we can challenge ourselves to find a way to meet our kids there, across the generational and cultural divide, rather than challenging them always to come to us. They inhabit this digital world as natives; we have to meet them in their world, or at least in the middle, if we want to connect with them.

So how can we make an ally of technology when we're bringing mindfulness to young people, rather than fighting and resisting it?

First, consider those times you reach for your phone to check out as an opportunity for a short mindfulness practice to check in first. The beeps and buzzes of our devices can also be reminders to take a breath or check in with ourselves. Mark Epstein, a psychiatrist and writer, suggests sometimes *not* shutting off the cell phone when you meditate. Instead, just sit in meditation and notice the body's and the mind's reactions to each beep and buzz of the phone, the stories and urges and emotions as they arise. The objects of attention become our emotional response to the silence (anticipation, relief), our emotional response to the beeps, chirps, songs, and buzzes as they arise (irritation, curiosity, anxiety), and whatever urges arise due to the sounds.

We can build subtle reminders into our devices, such as making the background wallpaper some kind of reminder to breathe or check in. How many times a day do we type a password into our devices? This too can be a reminder if we make our password *breathe* or something similar.

Plenty of free websites, apps, and podcasts offer guided meditations and discussion of meditation as well. Other software and hardware teach basic mind–body principles through biofeedback and neurofeedback. Plug-ins for browsers can block certain websites and distractions for chosen lengths of time. And given what we know about variable-rate conditioning effects, it is critical to shut off automatic passive alerts and push notifications, and instead make the *active* choice to check in with messages and updates.

Almost everyone has a portable recording device on their smartphone or tablet. In individual therapy and in groups, I use my device to record the guided meditations and then email the recordings to kids, post them on my website, or post them on a group blog where the kids can discuss them and interact. Kids often find something intimate and reassuring about a familiar voice guiding them through a practice, especially when the practice has been tailor-made for them. This way, they can carry us with them.

What other ways can you think of to meet kids in the digital world and engage them in mindfulness?

TIPS FOR HARNESSING TECHNOLOGY FOR MINDFULNESS PRACTICE

- Share practices with others in a social media group.

- Set your phone or tablet background image, your notification tone, or your passwords to be a reminder to practice some aspect of mindfulness.

- Record and listen to guided meditations on your devices.

- Set clear limits around screen time for yourself and your kids.

- Use your calendar and reminder functions to remind you to practice.

- Text or message practice reminders to friends or family members.

Social Media and the Comparing Mind

A flower does not compare itself to the other flowers. It just blossoms.
ANONYMOUS

Any social encounter, but particularly an encounter on social media, exacerbates the *comparing mind,* which is the cause of much unhappiness in individualist societies. The perfectly curated images posted of people's lives online means we are comparing our insides to other people's outsides. Certainly, adolescents have compared themselves to peers for generations, spending hours in front of the mirror and picking outfits for school, and are actually hardwired for self-consciousness. But the constant comparing and curating of the self-image used to end with the final bell of the school day, when kids could go home and put on their sweatpants. Today, with social media, keeping up appearances is a twenty-four-hour-a-day job; socializing and social comparison begin first thing in the morning and end last thing at night. Meanwhile, gossip sites broadcast nasty scrawls, once relegated to the bathroom wall, to the whole world. Psychology research consistently shows that social media is making kids unhappier and more narcissistic. The sheer volume and instant nature of digital media also means that when we log in, we are drinking from a fire hose of emotional stimulus. Take Facebook, for example: we can log in from anywhere in the world and be met by friends' posts that trigger joy, resentment, sadness, laughter, grief, jealousy, and more—all within moments. We can take ourselves on the same roller coaster by scanning news aggregators or other websites. Humans evolved in small social circles, and we are not wired to take in that much emotional content at once, much less to be triggered to go emotionally up and down and around, with no time to process and respond rather than react.

I was speaking with a young woman recently who was devastated by what someone wrote about her online. Naively, I asked, "Why don't you just not read that website?" She gave me one look and I knew the idea was an absolute nonstarter. So much socializing is happening online, and the fear of missing out, both online and in the real world, dominates the adolescent mind.

So, can we teach ourselves and the young people around us to approach social media feeds with mindfulness, even occasionally?

WHAT SCIENCE CAN TELL US ABOUT SOCIAL MEDIA

The science of social media is actually more complex than you might think. For example, research shows that the more we look at others' carefully curated Facebook status, the worse we tend to feel. But, the opposite is also true: if we look back at our own updates, we often see the positive aspects of our life presented and tend to feel better. So consider scrolling through your own updates sometimes, as you look at everyone else's.

Research also proves that social rewards and punishments are the same online and off. If someone interacts with us in a positive way, we get the same neurochemical rewards in the brain. When we (or our children) are rejected or ignored online, we get the same feeling of rejection as we would in person. More interestingly, the sense of emotional attack activates the same part of the brain as physical attack does. Emotional pain is just as painful, just as real, as physical pain.[3]

Mindful Social Media

Yes, social media is contributing to a new era of adolescent social stress, but when we accept that it is here to stay, we can also see it as a new opportunity for connection and mindfulness, *if we build it.* Mindfulness tells us there is insight to be found in anything when we approach it with mindfulness, and that even includes social media.

We can capture some of the power of community through social media. We can create mindfulness practice groups, and connect people to meditation teachers, mindfulness resources, and one another. Free blogging software makes uploading content and facilitating conversations in the hours of the week outside mindfulness group meeetings incredibly simple.

I am part of gratitude group on Facebook that began years ago with a dozen local friends. Many of us have moved away to other states and even continents, but we still check in with short lists of what we are grateful for a few times a week. Twitter, Instagram, and other sites make use of various meditation-related hashtags, such as *#wannasit,* or you can send compassion with a *#mettabomb* hashtag. Tumblr and other blogging sites allow us to share our experiences, favorite quotes, videos, and more. We can plan virtual sitting meditation sessions with friends across the country or around the world on days we can't plan a sit with a local friend. One of the simplest uses of technology is a group text message thread that I'm on with friends from my Sunday sitting medi-tation group. We just text an update when we've sat during the rest of the week, reply with happy emojis, and are inspired (or guilt-tripped) by one another's dedication. Young people might do something similar with a Snapchat list or via some other app that I don't understand.

Finally, here's a social media mindfulness practice to try yourself and then introduce to the kids you work with.

Find a comfortable, alert, and ready posture. Shrug your shoulders, take a few breaths, and bring aware-ness to your physical and emotional state in this particular moment.

Now open your computer or click on your phone.

Before you open up your favorite social media site, consider your intentions and expectations. As you focus on the icon, notice what experiences you have in your mind and body.

Why are you about to check this site? What are you hoping to see or not see? How are you going to respond to different kinds of updates you encounter? By checking your social media, are you interested in connecting or in disconnecting and distracting?

Close your eyes and focus on your emotional state for three breaths as you wait for the homepage or the app to open.

Opening your eyes now, look at the first status update or photo, and then sit back and close your eyes again.

Notice your response—your emotion. Is it excitement? Boredom? Jealousy? Regret? Fear? How do you experience this emotion in the mind and body? What's the urge—to read on, to click a response, to share yourself, or something else?

Wait a breath or two for the sensations and emotions to fade, or focus on your breath, body, or surrounding sounds, perhaps with a mindful moment practice.

Try this practice with one social media update, or for three or five minutes, depending on your time and your practice.

∪

Technology does not define us, despite social media trying to put us into categories and reduce us to a series of likes and interests. A Zen koan asks, "What did your face look like before you were born?" Today we might ask, "What did your Facebook page look like before you signed up?" It's the deep question of who you really are, beyond a series of quantifiable interests and algorithms. Examining and changing our own relationship to technology opens the door for us to teach through example and to practice new ways of making technology spiritual. We can even consider ways to make spiritual technology for the young people who are growing up natives in the connected world.

CHAPTER 11

making mindfulness stick
integrating short practices into the day

Mindfulness isn't difficult; we just need to remember to do it.

SHARON SALZBERG, *Real Happiness*

∪

Asking kids to practice mindfulness on their own may feel like a leap of faith. Our own self-doubt may return: Will they ever do this on their own? If they do, will they want to talk about it? Will their friends make fun of them? Again, trust the practices, trust yourself, and most of all, trust them. Create the space for growth but do not force it. If your kids are really resisting independent practice, just continue practicing together with them and cultivate mindfulness within the larger community, while returning to the well of your own practice.

The key to encouraging independent practice is to keep it both simple and fun. Recently I heard someone say, "You have to breathe and walk anyway. You might as well try to make it interesting." By some reports, we breathe up to 30,000 times a day, so we can probably make at least a few of those more mindful. If you are with a group of kids, the social reinforcement may help, as kids will likely want to join the follow-up discussion and share their experiences. This is especially true if they can express themselves creatively, through artwork, writing, or singing. I like to joke, "When the homework is to do nothing, it can't be that bad." We can also bring mindful attention to parts of the daily routine, like walking and eating, and we can break automatic habits—by, for example, brushing teeth with the nondominant hand—or find short, simple practices to integrate into life.

Factors like kids' experience, attention span, learning style, and existing mental or physical conditions, along with the culture and setting you're in, come into play when deciding what practices to suggest.

Short Moments, Many Times

> The moment . . . doesn't last very long by itself, but that's perfectly okay. You don't have to try to prolong that moment; rather, repeat it many times—"short moments, many times."
>
> LAMA TULKU URGYEN RINPOCHE, *As It Is*

We don't necessarily have time for extended mindfulness practices every day, but using short practices throughout the day will reinforce the lessons of our longer practices. Many of the short practices in this chapter are good ones for kids to do independently. The idea is to help kids bring short check-in practices into their daily lives at key or easy-to-remember times.

STOP AND TAKE A CUE FROM DAILY LIFE

Together with your kids, pick one or two regular times of day or signals to be reminder times, and one or two practices to do during those times, and build from there.

A number of years ago I worked with a teenage girl named Allegra, who had tremendous anxiety about school. She often missed the first few periods of the day because of stomachaches and anxiety, especially if math was the first class. Our goal was to find a way for her to make contact with the present moment and check in with herself and her mood, and then find a way for her to relax on the way to school, to make the day ahead more manageable. The practice time we picked was her walk to school and, more specifically, the times she encountered stop signs along the way. These signs became her reminders to check in mindfully with her experience and calm herself. The practice was simple: at every stop sign she would do the mindful STOP practice, which was popularized by Elisha Goldstein.

STOP is a quick acronym practice. Though it takes easily less than a minute, it enables us to mindfully check in with ourselves and our surroundings. At every stop sign, Allegra would:

stop what she was doing (assuming it was safe to do so),
take a breath,
observe what was happening, including what was happening inside her and what was happening around her, then
plan what to do next, and **proceed** with the activity.

The STOP practice didn't completely resolve Allegra's anxiety, but as she slowed down, she was able to bring more awareness to her anxiety in the present moment. If her anxiety was high on a particular day, Allegra would do a breathing practice or another self-soothing practice to help lower it, and then continue her walk to school. She's now in college and doing well, attending all of her classes, and she has even passed her math requirement.

On mindfulness retreats with Thich Nhat Hanh, a bell is rung every so often as a reminder to take three mindful breaths. After a few days, everyone automatically begins mindful breathing at the sound of the mindfulness bell. (For a few weeks after the retreat, the sound of any bell has the same effect.)

I did play therapy a few years ago with one charming seven-year-old girl who was curious about the meditation chimes I keep on my desk (a good reason to leave them out). We decided that if, at any point in the session, she got up and rang the bell, I would take three deep breaths, and she would take one. At first I thought she might get silly or distracted by the chimes, and she would occasionally. But for the most part, she took them seriously, and we had even more fun in our sessions. Her mom agreed to try the mindfulness chimes practice at home when they are playing together.

Ron Epstein, a researcher and mindfulness practitioner I saw speak recently, told us, "Between patients, when you open the door, touch the doorknob mindfully. Repeat ten thousand times." Inspired by this suggestion, another young woman I work with, who deals with chronic mild anxiety, uses the doorknob as a reminder to check in with her body and mind. Her practice is to notice how her body feels every time she touches a doorknob when leaving a room and to check in with how her mind and emotions feel every time she enters a room. We joke that on stressful days she drinks a lot of water to make sure she needs to go to the bathroom a few extra times, giving her more opportunities to leave and enter rooms.

The point is, if you or your kids think you don't have time for even a little mindfulness practice, think again. There are endless little moments in our everyday lives that we can make into mindfulness cues or mindful moments. Below is a list of 101.

The temptation is to choose a lot of moments, but I encourage you to pick just one or two, pair them with a simple informal practice for a week or so, and build from there. Keep in mind that new practices are most likely to stick when they are connected to activities that the kid is already doing as part of their routine.

Kids can take an opportunity to be mindful whenever they are reminded by the following:

1. Lying in bed first thing in the morning, just before getting up

2. Waiting for the bathtub to fill or the shower to warm up

3. Sitting at a stoplight

4. Riding between stations on the subway

5. While attendance is taken at school

6. Waiting for a video game to load

7. Waiting for a website to load or an application to open

8. Waiting for the toast to pop out of the toaster, or the microwave to chime

9. Sitting in a time out

10. Waiting for the bus, the subway, or a ride

11. Waiting to stand up at the end of a flight or bus ride

12. Waiting for everyone else to arrive in a room or at a table

13. Sitting in a waiting room

14. Waiting for the printer to print

15. Standing in line

16. Waiting for the Wi-Fi to connect

17. Waiting for a computer to start up

18. Waiting for their turn in a game

19. Waiting for the gas tank of the car to fill

20. Waiting for coffee to brew or tea to steep

21. Waiting for advertisements on TV or a website video to end

22. Waiting for a chat or reply from a friend

23. Waiting to cross the street

24. Dropping a letter into a mailbox

They might pause for a short mindfulness practice every time they:

25. Walk through a doorway

26. Hear the sound of a text message

27. Hear the chime of a social media alert

28. Hear birds chirping

29. See a certain color you or they have chosen for the day or week

30. Hear a particular word you or they have chosen for the day or week

31. Touch a doorknob

32. See brake lights on the freeway

33. Stand at the bottom of a staircase

34. Hear the ring of a phone

35. Pass a specific landmark, like a certain beautiful tree, on a regular walk or drive

36. Touch a light switch

37. Walk or drive by a stop sign

38. See or hear an airplane flying overhead

39. Hear car horns blare in the distance

40. Feel wind on their cheek

41. Turn a faucet handle

42. Hear an emergency siren (this also can be an opportunity for a compassion or kind wishes practice)

43. Hear the sound of laughter

44. Glimpse the moon during the daytime

45. Look at their watch or a clock

46. Hear the beeps of a truck backing up

47. Hear the refrigerator or furnace click on

48. Hear the sound of a car starting

49. Take out their dog's leash or head out with their dog for a walk

50. Plug in or unplug something

51. Sit, stand, or transition between two body positions

52. Give someone a handshake, fist bump, or high five

53. Hear a car alarm in the distance

54. Click a pen

55. See an annoying popup ad

56. Hear their dog bark or their cat meow

57. Put their feet on the floor as they get out of bed

58. Hear the ding of the doorbell

59. Open their wallet

60. Open a book or notebook

61. Notice a certain smell, such as the smell of flowers

62. Hear the sound of a crying baby (this is another good opportunity for a compassion practice)

63. Feel their hand creeping toward their phone

64. See you—their parent, teacher, therapist—hear your voice, pass by your office, or get a message from you

65. Score a point in a game—or having one scored on them

Kids can pause and do a short practice, such as taking a mindful breath or doing a body scan, just before they:

66. Open the lock on their locker

67. Press Play on their iPod

68. Step into a shower stall or bathtub

69. Press an elevator button

70. Open the fridge or a cabinet

71. Put a key in a lock

72. Press the On button on anything

73. Open an envelope

74. Start a walk or hike

75. Open their bag

76. Take the first bite of a meal

77. Settle into homework

78. Click on the TV

79. Feed their pet

80. Press Send on an email or text message

81. Sign their name

You or your kids can designate certain small, everyday actions to be done with mindfulness, such as:

82. Walking a pet

83. Refilling a glass or a water bottle

84. Placing something into the recycling/trash/compost bin

85. Peeling an orange or banana

86. Walking from a parking lot into a building

87. Walking down a hallway

88. Swiping a credit card or subway card

89. Hugging or cuddling someone

90. Loading the laundry into the washer or dryer

91. Putting on socks or tying their shoes

92. Fastening a seatbelt

93. Sharpening a pencil

94. Shaking hands with someone

95. Putting a stamp on a letter

96. Putting money into a vending machine

It can be helpful to do a short mindfulness or self-compassion practice right before any anxiety-producing situation, such as:

97. A big game or performance

98. Walking into a busy cafeteria, classroom, or party

99. Before public speaking

100. Waiting for the teacher to hand out exams

101. Lying in bed at night, waiting to fall asleep

I'm sure you and your kids can easily think of dozens more cues or reminders to pause and be mindful during your everyday lives. And here's a way to look for them: just notice any time you feel that urge to reach for your phone and check out, and take a moment to mindfully check in first. You can also set alerts on your phones or computers.

TIPS FOR CHOOSING CUES OR MINDFUL MOMENTS

When you're starting out, it's helpful to have a consistent time or cue signaling you to do short check-ins with yourself and with your kids. Routine is helpful for kids, as parents and teachers know, and practice at transition times can help. If you work with kids professionally, maybe that means the start or end of a class, activity, or session. When the practices are part of the daily routine and larger culture, kids begin to internalize them. Most importantly, they don't see practicing mindfulness as weird, and they don't associate practice with punishment or a problem because they've already practiced in hard times and good times.

There are good times of day for practice, but finding the ideal emotional times for mindfulness practice can be challenging. Knowing the emotional rhythms of your kid is important. We want to introduce these practices to the most open mind possible, and the mind is rarely open when we are emotional. When someone is in fight-or-flight mode or otherwise emotionally flooded, there is minimal bandwidth for taking in information that isn't related to immediate survival, whether it's information about mindfulness or math. Most kids understand that athletes, musicians, or other performers don't train only on the day of the competition or concert, but practice and work out for months or years before the big event. Mindfulness practice is like working out for the mind. And in fact, research is showing that even a few moments of daily mindfulness practice is probably better than long stretches of practice done less often.

Short Practices

There are dozens of practices that take a minute or less. The short practices that follow teach elements of mindfulness: awareness, present moment contact, compassion/curiosity. They include check-in and relaxation practices and body, breath, and mental practices.

Different practices will suit different kids or may feel more natural than others. Breath practices can be hard for anxious kids or those with attention issues; movement practices or practices that use external anchors might be preferable. Body awareness can be very helpful, but it's not an ideal starting point for kids who have negative associations with their body, perhaps from illness, trauma, or body image concerns. Relaxation techniques for the mind and body may be great for stress or anxiety, but are not as helpful for kids who are tired or depressed.

You might put the instructions for one of these short practices up on the wall and make it the practice of the day or week, or have kids carry instructions on a notecard or in their phone. To integrate mindfulness into daily life, read through the list of 101 moments, then help your kid match the chosen moment to one of these short practices.

SOUP BREATHING

Breathing can be boring and, admittedly, hard to make more interesting. But metaphors and visualizations can help. A participant in a workshop I gave introduced me to Soup Breathing, an easily adapted visualization that teaches regulated breathing.

> Hold out your hands as if you were holding a bowl of soup up to your face. Breathe in gently through your nose as if you are breathing in the delicious smell of the soup. Breathe out through your lips as if you are blowing across the surface of the full bowl of soup to cool it, but not so hard that it spills.

I've done borscht breathing in Poland, tea breathing in England, and porridge breathing in Bhutan. In the U.S. I've done hot chocolate breathing and even pizza breathing. I'm sure you and your kids can together think of more favorites. With beginners or to quickly calm the mind and body, try doing just five soup breaths; with experienced kids, try a few minutes' worth.

Research in biofeedback suggests that visualization alone can warm our hands, which in turn relaxes the nervous system. What better way to warm your hands than by visualizing a bowl of soup or a mug of hot chocolate? You can also call this the "cooling off breath," because what better way is there to cool off your "hot" emotions, like anger and frustration, than by feeling cool air rushing out of your mouth?

THE 7–11 BREATH

Resetting the breath with a deliberate practice can regulate, shift, and stabilize energy and mood. Another short, sweet, easy-to-remember practice is the 7–11 Breath. Most of us know 7-Eleven as the name of a convenience store chain, and if you pass one of these stores regularly, you can let that be a cue to do this practice. I learned it at a training with the Mindfulness in Schools Project, and since then I have read that first responders use it to keep themselves and others calm in emergencies. Telling a few of your challenging skeptics that even tough firefighters and ambulance drivers use this breath practice might persuade them to use it.

The directions are simple:

> Breathe *in* for a count of seven.
> Breathe *out* for a count of eleven.

The 7–11 Breath can be done five breaths at a time when kids are learning it, and then longer, depending on how much time you have. This one requires a little more practice than the Soup Breath, to get the counting right, so give kids a chance to learn it. The counting also forces kids (and adults) to focus more and to slow it down—before I knew some of these practices, I'd suggest deep breathing and I'd get kids breathing really deep, but also really fast. Often, what we really mean is slow breathing, not deep breathing. Making the exhale longer than the inhale relaxes the nervous system and allows us to make contact with the present when we might otherwise be rushing past it.

And the opposite is also true: making the inhale longer than the exhale jump-starts the nervous system and speeds us up. In low energy situations—when we find ourselves feeling worn out, sluggish, or a little depressed, and want to raise our energy to meet the present moment—try an 11–7 Breath: the opposite ratio.

My friend Adria Kennedy, who teaches mindfulness to kids, adapts this practice for younger kids by asking them to breathe words or phrases in and out. For example, try breathing in for the length of the word *Maine* and breathing out *Massachusetts,* or breathe in *bird* and breathe out *brontosaurus.*

THE SILENT SIGH

A sigh can mean many things—relief, exasperation, pleasure, exhaustion, even sadness. Physiologically, sighing regulates and resets our breathing rate. Kids and adults sigh unconsciously, and we can unintentionally offend others when we do so. The Silent Sigh is a deliberate and respectful way of sighing. I learned it from Irene McHenry, an educator and fellow board member at the Mindfulness in Education Network.

This practice allows us to let out excess emotion and reset our body and breath. For that reason, it can be good for settling back into the present moment during transition times.

Take a deep breath in. Then let out a sigh as slowly and silently as possible, so that no one even knows you are doing it.

Follow along with all the sensations in your body as you breathe out to the last bit of air in your body. Then check in with how your mind and body feel. Decide if you need another silent sigh, or just let your breath return to normal.

I like to start by inviting kids to try a loud regular sigh to demonstrate how it feels to let out their emotions in a sigh (and to have some fun). Then I shift to the Silent Sigh and explain that there are situations when it might be more appropriate than a regular sigh, such as in a classroom or when we do not want to offend people by sighing at them.

BREATHING WITH ALL OUR SENSES

Using our senses is often the fastest way to become present and aware of what we are doing. In this mindful breathing practice, we use all of our senses to bring awareness to the breath.

> As you take the next few breaths, use all of your senses to notice that you are breathing.
>
> On the first breath, what does the breath sound like?
>
> On the next breath, what does the breath feel like?
>
> As you breathe again, what does the air of the breath smell like?
>
> As you breathe once more, what does the air of the breath taste like?
>
> Lastly, what does the breath look like?
>
> If you watch the last breath closely, you might notice how your head and body shift ever so slightly with the in-breath and the out-breath. Or you might see what the breath looks like by imagining how the breath looks going down into the belly.
>
> Keep breathing through your senses until you've done each sense three times.

FIVE-FINGER BREATHING

I learned this practice at a training for the Mindfulness in Schools Project, and it fast became one of my personal and professional favorites for self-soothing. Another breath-regulation practice, it uses touch, counting, and breathing as anchors.

Hold out one hand, fingers spread, palm facing toward you.

Rest the index finger of your other hand on the base of the thumb of the outstretched hand.

As you take a slow in-breath, slowly run your finger up one side of your thumb and count "one." As you reach the top of your thumb, you should finish the in-breath.

From there, start the out-breath and count "two" as you run your finger down the other side of your thumb.

When your finger reaches the bottom point between the extended thumb and forefinger, inhale again and move up the side of the extended index finger as you count "three." Then exhale and move down the other side of the extended forefinger as you count "four."

Continue inhaling and exhaling and tracing each finger of the extended hand until you reach ten, on the down-side of your pinkie.

Variations include using a stopwatch and counting how many or few breaths can be done in a minute. Kids can also switch hands for counting and notice the differences between hands.

THE FOUR-SQUARE BREATH

The Four-Square Breath is another way to regulate or reset the breath when it is out of a natural, easy rhythm. A few breaths in and out with a count to four evens it out. Kids can move their hands in a square as they count each breath.

 Breathe in for a count of four.

Hold for a count of four.

Breathe out for a count of four.

Hold for a count of four.

Repeat three times and then allow the breath to find its own rhythm.

Holding the breath can produce anxiety in some kids, so the 7–11 Breath or Soup Breathing may be better for them than this practice. Do what works and feels comfortable.

METTA (LOVINGKINDNESS) BREATH

This practice may not be ideal for a public situation, but for young kids in a group or alone, it can be fun and feels good. My friend Samu Sundquist and I came up with this together while doing a workshop in Helsinki.

> Sitting or standing, with your arms at your sides, take a deep in-breath.
>
> On the out-breath, expand your arms as wide as possible, as if you were hugging the entire world, fitting in absolutely everybody you can.
>
> On the next in-breath, bring your arms in and hug yourself, arms reaching across the chest, each hand on the opposite shoulder.
>
> On the next out-breath, open your arms wide again, hugging and comforting the whole world.
>
> Take another in-breath and bring your arms in, hugging and comforting yourself.

Start by doing the Metta Breath five times in a row and see how you feel afterward. The next time you do it, you can take more or fewer breaths, according to what you need or the time available.

THE SPACE BETWEEN

Sometimes focusing on the breath itself is a challenge or leads to anxiety. In those cases, it can be helpful to see that there is a space of stillness between our breaths—"the Still Quiet Place," as my friend Amy Saltzman calls it. Try to find your still place between the breaths for five breaths.

Just allow yourself to breathe. As you do, find the spaces of stillness where the in-breath turns into the out-breath and the out-breath turns into the in-breath. Rest your attention on these spaces for a few breaths.

THE BUTTERFLY HUG

This soothing emotional-regulation practice was developed for child survivors of natural disasters, and mimics the flapping of butterfly wings.

Find a comfortable position—sitting, standing, or lying down.

Now, just hug yourself, arms across the chest, each hand on the opposite shoulder.

Take a few moments to gently tap or squeeze your shoulders in alternating rhythm—left right, left right.

SENSORY SCAN

One of the best and quickest ways back to the present moment is through our five senses.

Calm your body, find a still posture, and close your eyes.

First, notice physical sensations. A mole cannot see, but it has a strong sense of touch, feeling the sensations and vibrations of its environment. Scan the edges of your body. Notice the sensations on your skin, such as those made by your clothing or the air. Feel deeper inside your body, to your muscles and organs, and notice what you can sense.

Now, notice sounds. A deer's ears are among the most powerful of any animal. Can you listen like a deer? Can you hear any sound at this very moment, near or far?

Then, switch to smell. A dog, or a wolf, has a powerful sense of smell that gives it information about

the world. Smell like a wolf. As you breathe in through
your nose, what smells do you notice? Perhaps food
cooking in the distance, the smell of fresh air, or
someone's perfume nearby?

Focus on the sense of taste. A catfish is said to
have the most powerful sense of taste of any animal.
Open your mouth a little bit. Can you taste anything
in the environment? What tastes linger in your mouth
or on your tongue after you close your mouth?

Now open your eyes. What's in your field of
vision at this very moment? Eagles have strong eyes
that can zoom in to see a small animal from high
above. And small animals take in all their surroundings in order to watch for predators. See if you can
take in everything around you, or just focus in on
something beautiful.

Welcome to the here and now.

In Eastern psychologies, there are not five senses but six. You can add
the sixth one, the mind or thought sense, to the practice, if you like.

A variation, which I learned from author Dawn Huebner, suggests
first paying attention to the first thing you notice with each sense,
then noticing what else is there in the background. This reminds us
how much more is going on beyond what we are at first aware of. Or,
instead of using animal senses, try using superhero supersenses.

3-2-1 CONTACT

This practice is an informal complement to the Settling Practice in
chapter 5.

 Notice three places where your body makes contact with
the world. Your feet, legs, and arms are obvious ones,
but also notice your skin meeting the air or touching the
fabric of your clothes.

Jennifer Cohen Harper teaches a variation which she calls the Desk Practice, in which you notice feet on the floor, legs on the chair, and arms on the desk or table in front of you, gently pressing on each to feel more grounded.

SLOW DOWN

My friend Mitch Abblett suggests slowing down in our bodies and minds. He does this between his meetings with families. He remembers his process with the acronym SLOW:

Soften your face and body.
Lower your shoulders.
Open your chest and belly with a breath.
Wilt your fingers and hands.

I love the idea of mindfulness as just slowing down. A friend of mine pointed out recently that we compliment kids and one another on how fast we get things done, but when was the last time someone complimented you on how slowly you did something?

HALT

When I was working as a substance abuse counselor, my colleagues and I would remind people to take care of their basic needs in order to be strong enough to handle triggers and urges that appear when we are most vulnerable. This quick scan of our emotional and physical experience is summed up by the acronym HALT.

Quickly check in with yourself. Are you feeling:
- **hungry**
- **angry (and/or anxious)**
- **lonely**
- **tired**

If you are feeling any of these, what can you do to respond to your own needs and take care of yourself?

Hunger, anger, anxiety, loneliness, and tiredness are some of the most basic human experiences; in fact, besides a wet diaper, these are the most likely reasons that a baby is crying! We grownups are not always so different in our basic needs.

THINK BEFORE YOU SPEAK

Many children, and we adults too, struggle with being impulsive in our speech—and, in the digital age, in our emails, texts, and instant messages as well. I've seen variations of this helpful acronym in a few places, from kindergartens to meditation centers.

Before you speak, pause and ask yourself:
- Is what I am about to say **true?**
- Is this going to be **helpful?**
- Am I the one to say it? Or, is it **inspiring?**
- Is **now** the time to say it? And, is it **necessary?**
- Is what I am about to say **kind?**

SEEKING STILLNESS

When the world is spinning inside, it can help to look for examples of stillness outside.

Find some stillness in the world around you—perhaps a building, a boulder, a statue, the base of a tree, or something else unmoving. Rest your awareness there and breathe for a few moments until you can connect that external stillness with a stillness inside.

SHADES OF GREEN

A few summers ago, I was hiking around a lake in springtime and looking across at the green forest on the other side, when I realized that there must be dozens of shades of green. I took a moment and started counting them until I lost count. Noticing the green of life in the winter, when the world looks bleak, or at any time of year, is a quick way to ground yourself and be aware of your surroundings.

I like looking for green because to me it symbolizes thriving life, but you can use other colors too. Since sharing this practice with others, I've learned that the human eye can discern more shades of green than any other color. I was doing this practice on a retreat last summer while doing mindful walking, and suddenly, out of the green, a seven-leaf clover popped into my vision. You never know what you might discover when you look at the world in different ways.

In one of the Jataka tales about the Buddha, he was reincarnated as a deer, which was captured along with its entire herd by an evil king. When the other members of the herd became fearful, the Buddha deer reminded them that as long as the blue sky was above them and the green grass was below them, they should not despair, because wherever there is life there is hope. Just tuning into all that is alive around us, particularly in the darkness of winter, can help us gain a hopeful perspective as well.

SIFTING OUR EXPERIENCE

Developmental psychiatrist Daniel Siegel uses a simple acronym for the four steps of a practice to check in with our experience in the present moment.[1]

> Take a breath and mindfully notice what is happening in your experience in the present moment in terms of:
> - **Sensations** in the body
> - **Images** or movies in the mind
> - **Feelings** and emotions
> - **Thoughts** occurring in the mind

SIFTing our experience a few times a day builds the habit of noticing what our experience really is in the present moment, which strengthens the muscle of awareness. It's also a useful way to ask kids to reflect after a practice; you can ask what came up for them in these four realms during the practice.

SCANS YOUR BODY

The acronym SCANS makes this mini body-scan practice easy to remember. SCANS stands for stomach, chest, arms, neck, and shoulders, the parts of the body that tend to give us the most information about our emotions. Kids can write "SCANS" as a reminder on their binder, in their planner, or another place they see often.

 Check in with your **stomach.** Is it relaxed, nervous, tight, fluttery? Is your breath close to your stomach?

Check in with your **chest.** Is it tight or relaxed? How is your heartbeat? Is your breath up in your chest?

Check in with your **arms.** Are they tense or relaxed? Are your hands making fists or gently resting?

Check in with your **neck.** Is there soreness or achiness, or does it feel relaxed?

Last, check in with your **shoulders.** Are they hunched or resting?

THE NAGGING FEELING

This practice can be helpful for dealing with yucky feelings. It reminds kids that yucky feelings come, but they also eventually leave—that all feelings are impermanent. The acronym NAG represents the three steps.

Notice what feelings are here.
Allow them to visit.
Then watch them **go.**

This is similar to a practice by Michele McDonald called RAIN, which stands for *recognize, allow, investigate,* and *nonidentify.*

SENSATION COUNTDOWN

This practice helps us gather our attention and settle our thoughts before beginning work or a task that requires focus.

 Notice a sensation at the edge of your body, where your skin meets the world.

Notice a sensation somewhere in your body, just under your skin.

Notice a sensation deeper inside your body.

SOUND COUNTDOWN

This is another listening practice. For more listening and sound practices, see chapter 8. Like the Sensation Countdown, it can help us gather and focus on the task at hand, be it in the classroom, before homework, or something else that requires attention.

 Notice a sound outside the building you are in.

Notice a sound inside the building.

Notice a sound inside the room.

Notice a sound landing and vibrating on or in your body.

Notice a sound inside your body. Try covering your ears if you like. Maybe it's your thoughts.

ZOOM LENS AND WIDE LENS

I've also heard this practice called Predator Eyes and Prey Eyes, which seems a little scary, but maybe it could be Eagle Eyes and Mouse Eyes. Think about what imagery works best for you.

For a few breaths, focus on just one object in your surroundings. Then expand your field of vision to take in the
whole of your surroundings.

Keep shifting your focus between zoom lens and wide-
angle after every few breaths.

From there, try to zoom in and out on thoughts or
emotions in your mind and body.

You can do a variation of this practice with sounds, focusing in on
one sound for a few breaths, then zooming out to listen to the entire
soundscape at once.

THE COLOR DETECTIVE

Teddy, one of my elementary school-aged clients, came up with this
practice. He volunteers to read to the kindergarteners at his school and
now shares mindfulness practices with them as well.

 Look around the room for each color of the rainbow. When
you see each color, breathe it in and move on to the next.

SEEING WITH DIFFERENT EYES

The breath and body are great shortcuts back to the present moment,
but we can also use our eyes to become present and increase awareness
and perspective. These three short visual practices are good for kids of
any age.

 Samurai's Eyes: Gaze around the room and try to
memorize what everything looks like. Close your eyes
and try to reconstruct what you saw in a mental image.
When you open them again, see how close you were.

Child's Eyes: Look around the room with fresh
eyes and beginner's mind, even if it's a place you

know well. Keep looking until you see something
you have never noticed before.

Artist's Eyes: Gaze around the room and notice the
objects. Then stop focusing on the objects and instead
notice the space around them—the negative space, as
artists call it.

JUST BE X 3

This is an adaptation of a shorter practice from Elisha Goldstein's 2015
book *Uncovering Happiness*.[2] Each pair of lines encourages us to just be
by making use of the acronym BE.

Breathe in,
Expand your body.
Breathe in,
Expand your mind.
Breathe in,
Expand your view.

KIND WISHES

This is a simple lovingkindness practice that offers kind wishes to ourselves, as well as to people in our world. (For more on lovingkindness,
or *metta*, see chapter 13.) Some kids might find it hard to make a
wish for someone they don't like, so maybe a wish for the whole world
would work better for them.

Make a kind wish for yourself.
 Make a kind wish for a friend or family member.
 Make a kind wish for someone you don't know very well.
 And if you feel comfortable or brave, make a kind wish
for someone you don't like very much or who bothers you.

LIVING MINDFULLY: MAKING LIFE ITSELF THE ANCHOR OF MEDITATION

Spiritual practice is not just sitting and meditating. Practice is looking, thinking, touching, drinking, eating, and talking. Every act, every breath, and every step can be practice and can help us to become more ourselves.

THICH NHAT HANH, *Your True Home*

The work of integrating mindfulness into life is twofold: First, we can find times of day or cues to prompt us to do short practices. We can also bring mindful awareness to activities we are already doing, including playing, working, moving, and interacting with others, by using short practices such as How Do I Know?, in chapter 3. We can also use the "Four Rs" in whatever we are doing: *rest* our awareness on the task, *recognize* where and when it wanders, and then gently *return* to the task (and *repeat*). Integrating mindfulness into our lives is how we move toward making life itself the anchor of meditation.

How often do we or our kids operate on autopilot? As adults, are we on autopilot or are we aware of our interactions and speech? Can we teach our children to be more fully present, integrating mindfulness into not just therapy or the classrooms, but also art and creative expression, writing, movement, sports, and other parts of daily life?

When we are fully present with everything, we are happier. Recall the study described in chapter 2, which found that what we are doing is half as important to our happiness as whether we are focused on it. We can support our focus by cultivating mindfulness, but we can also subtract distractions and cut down on multitasking.

For kids, bringing mindfulness into everyday life might just look like a little more silence, a little more slowing down, and more one-thing-at-a-time built into the day's routines. In addition to reviewing the ideas given throughout part II, you can check out my previous book, *Child's Mind,* for a list of 100 activities for kids to do mindfully. Better yet, make your own list.

One of the joys of deeper mindfulness integration and more mindful living is that kids and adults together start to become *acculturated* to mindfulness through shared experience. We can share common insights and common frustrations that arise from the practice. Common experience leads to a common language we can use to speak about mindfulness: *sitting with that, allowing it to arise and pass,* and *dropping in* or *dropping anchor.* We can check in with each other by asking, "How's the weather in your mind this morning? What's the forecast?" or whatever metaphors and language have taken hold and are flowing through your family or community. This shared vocabulary reinforces and inspires the practice in everyone.

Ultimately, the intention is to truly live mindfully. But not many kids—in fact, not most kids—will get there, nor will many adults. In my early, grandiose years, I imagined everyone I worked with learning to live a perfectly mindful life. I forgot that it started with me living a perfectly mindful life. In the years since, I've revised my goals and tried to take my ego out of the equation. I let go of reaching that goal in the everyday world, and yet never stop aiming for it as an aspiration. We can still aim to teach others how to have a fully integrated formal and informal mindfulness practice even if we, as teachers, have yet to achieve that practice. Like enlightenment or sainthood in spiritual traditions, truly living mindfully can be a north star to navigate by and toward, but not necessarily to reach.

At our best, we and our kids can live this way sometimes, using mindfulness to see a situation clearly and to deal with it skillfully. Some days we may come closer than others, and self-compassion will help us through it all. Ideally, not only can children use mindfulness to observe their experience and choose wise actions, but they will also have the option of using mindfulness itself as the wise or skillful action. This is where we see transformation. Aware of their context and feeling the emotions originating in their body, they can see choices arise: *Do I drink, or do I walk away? Do I breathe through my fears and go onstage, or do I give up? Do I take a positive action and maybe use my mindfulness, or do I make a choice I'll later regret?*

PART III

sharing mindfulness
in a formal setting

CHAPTER 12

tips for teaching mindfulness

It is by teaching that we teach ourselves, by relating
that we observe, by affirming that we examine,
by showing that we look, by writing that we think,
by pumping that we draw water into the well.

HENRI-FRÉDÉRIC AMIEL, *Amiel's Journal*, 1882,
translated by Mary A. Ward

In sharing mindfulness and compassion with kids, there are challenges as well as rewards. There is no "one size fits all" when it comes to teaching. This chapter covers the basics of best practice for teaching kids mindfulness, compiled from my own experience and from discussions with leading colleagues. I include not only advice for generating interest and getting buy-in, but also techniques for facilitating conversation after a practice. This information will be helpful whether you are teaching your own child or working with children as a professional.

We play many roles with the kids in our lives: parents, teachers, therapists, friends, and more. I was a teacher for a few years before I became a psychologist, and now I am also a parent. Each role has shaped how I think about mindfulness and sharing mindfulness with kids. Kids probably spend more time in school than almost anywhere else; thus, educators have a unique opportunity to introduce kids to mindfulness. Historically, monasteries, in both the East and the West, were the places of learning; prayer and meditation taught people to concentrate effectively, to learn more effectively, and to think more creatively. Bringing mindfulness back into spaces of learning just makes sense.

If you are a therapist, you have unique opportunities to integrate mindfulness into your work with children. Mindfulness has been shown repeatedly to help with mental health and other struggles, and you have structured one-on-one time in which to teach and practice it. Mindfulness can help you if you are a nurse or a doctor who works with kids. Evidence shows that it helps you to be more focused, empathic, and effective, while helping your patients recover from illness and injury faster and more fully.

If you are a parent, you have plenty of opportunities to bring mindfulness and compassion to everything you do with your child, throughout their lives. Younger children may be more open than skeptical teens, who might not want to hear it from you. Fortunately, other adult mentors can share mindfulness practices with them. If their practice takes root, you might find your grown children eventually sharing practice with you, as I now do with my own parents.

Sustaining our own practice is often a challenge, but it's particularly challenging when we're also trying to share mindfulness practice with others. Traditionally, practice is sustained by three elements: solid teachings, inner motivation, and community support. In Buddhism, these elements are described as the three jewels: the *dharma*, the Buddha, and the *sangha*. These three elements enable a practice to grow and thrive over time. When we're sharing mindfulness with kids, good teaching, a supportive community, and the right techniques must match the kids' learning needs and tap into their intrinsic curiosity and motivation. Finding this sweet spot may seem like alchemy, but the best practices for teaching, which I share in this chapter, will help you get there.

HOW TO SUPPORT KIDS' DEVELOPING PRACTICE

It is helpful to consider the following steps and priorities as we support our kids' mindfulness practice:

1. Cultivate **our own practice.**

2. Create or join a **community** that supports our practice and that of young people.

3. Begin **formal instruction,** teaching kids and leading them in practices, as well as practicing with them.

4. Share **informal practices** to integrate mindfulness into everyday life.

5. Bring mindful awareness into **regular activities.**

This model also helps us with kids' resistance. At each step, if we encounter resistance, we can move back down the list to the previous step.

The Practice of Teaching

Many of us want to share mindfulness with young people because we've experienced the benefits ourselves. We've likely also experienced the challenges of bringing what we've learned on our meditation cushions into our daily lives. Even more challenging is translating that wisdom into teachings for kids, so that they can learn and grow from our practice and their own, and take the wisdom into their playgrounds, classrooms, families, and neighborhoods.

For many of us, going from practicing mindfulness to teaching mindfulness feels like a big step. It can be strange, after years of what for most people is a very personal practice, to start sharing it with others. It may raise feelings of insecurity and doubt: *I'm not good enough. Who am I to teach this? I'm not Thich Nhat Hanh! They'll laugh at me. I'll screw up!* This is especially true if we are sharing with teenagers, whose self-doubt, self-consciousness, judgment, and skepticism can be contagious (but is rarely fatal). If you have such feelings, you're not alone; doubts are common when we're starting out and common even after we've been teaching for a while. If you have doubts about your ability to lead a mindfulness practice, check in with your own meditation teacher or mentor. And if you have *no* doubts and feel supremely confident, then *definitely* check in with someone. Seeking guidance is not weakness. By asking for support when we need it, we are modeling humility for our children, while also demonstrating our interdependence.

The intention of this book is to help you plant the seeds of mindfulness in kids, which often means merely offering the experience of the basic elements of mindfulness—present moment contact, awareness, and focus, as well as acceptance and nonjudgment—or sharing what Susan Kaiser Greenland calls "the new ABCs": attention, balance, and compassion. When we have done that, we have done our job and met our intentions, whether a formal practice blossoms in the kids' lives or not.

Begin with Beginner's Mind

Approach teaching with a beginner's mind attitude about yourself, the setting, and about the kids. If you can, let go of preconceptions and expectations. Whether you are a parent expecting a fight (or even an eye roll), a teacher who just heard some gossip about the kids, or a therapist who just read a two-inch-thick case file before meeting a kid, try to meet the kids with open heart and mind. If you can be open-minded and open-hearted, the kids will feel safe enough to respond in kind. If you go in with a predetermined idea of how things will go, the kids will respond in kind, with closed minds and hearts. And if you can see the kids with beginner's mind, this perspective has a chance of spreading.

A pre-teaching ritual or practice will help you find your beginner's mind. Perhaps say some gentle self-compassion phrases, find a way of settling yourself, or make an effort to clear a space mentally, physically, and emotionally.

Maybe you are a parent or grandparent; maybe you are a therapist or a teacher; perhaps you play an entirely different role in the life of the kid to whom you wish to introduce mindfulness. It's easy for us, as adults, to forget what being a child is like, even though we've all shared the experience! If you can comfortably reconnect with the positive aspects of your own childhood, you will be able to connect more effectively and authentically with the kids you want to reach.

Leading Practices

Whether you lead practices in your living room, classroom, or office; work with breath awareness or creative expression; or teach joyful kindergarteners or juvenile convicts, the intention is the same: to engage the kids and offer a positive experience of mindfulness.

Starting with practices that resonate with you will up the odds of the practices resonating with the kids. Building up to a goal together—perhaps practicing for ten breaths or ten minutes—can inspire and motivate kids. The clearer we are with instructions, the easier they are to follow, and the safer and more comfortable kids feel.

For some kids, slowing down with mindfulness may be a relief; for others, it may be unfamiliar and uncomfortable; and for others, it may feel unsafe. Saying "We are going to sit quietly with our thoughts" can sound boring, ambiguous, or even scary, depending on the child. Silence has different meanings in different contexts and cultures. In therapy, silence often means a healing space, but in school or in families, it can signal danger, trouble, or loneliness. On the other hand, instructions such as "We are going to sit for one minute and just listen to all the sounds we can hear, and then we're going to discuss what we noticed" are both clear and containing. Starting with a concrete practice such as listening to sounds, rather than starting with an abstract practice such as noticing thoughts, is a way for kids to feel successful and to keep their motivation up. Definitions of mindfulness—of which there are many variations for kids—should be clear and concise. A good rule of thumb is that the definition should be simple enough for a kid to explain to family members or friends.

You may need to loosen your attachment to what meditation looks like for you. For kids, meditation might not mean eyes closed, back straight, or feet on the floor—positions that can feel unfamiliar, uncomfortable, unsafe, or have different meaning in different cultures. Asking kids to close or lower their eyes helps to alleviate distraction as well as self-consciousness, but again, know your kids; some may find that uncomfortable.

Length of meditation time is also going to be different. A good length is what your kids can tolerate until they begin squirming, plus a tiny bit more. Longer seated meditations are often easier when we're in a certain posture, and so rather than explain the "right" or "wrong" way to sit, I just say, "The best posture is one you can maintain for a while without getting uncomfortable or sleepy. For me, that's sitting upright." The stance becomes an invitation, rather than a command, which is fundamentally different from what most kids get at school and at home. Rather than saying, "Sitting longer is better," I invite kids to sit more by saying, "Sitting for longer times or more often means more opportunities to notice your thoughts."

Your flexible but supportive attitude gets away from the predictable dichotomy of right and wrong that many kids live in. It helps simply to let go of your own attachment to what meditation *should* be. These preconceived ideas come out of cultural traditions which may not align with those of the kids you're working with. Rather than showing up with a rigid curriculum and expecting the kids to adapt, it is better for us to adapt ourselves and our practices to suit their minds, bodies, and spirits.

When possible, practice alongside the kids. The kids may or may not do the practice themselves, but you are still teaching them in the moment, with your presence, to be fully present for the time you are together. Although I don't always close my eyes when leading a meditation, I find it helpful to model a mindful posture, and by following along with a script, I can see what is working in the language. Practicing together demonstrates that you're not asking the kids to do anything you wouldn't do—which is also unlike the authority-figure dynamics that many kids are accustomed to. Of course, it's hard to talk with chocolate in your mouth during an eating meditation, and some movements of a movement practice might wear you out. In those cases, do everything you can while still leading.

Remember that, when you're starting out, the intention is just to introduce mindful awareness and set kids up for a positive experience. If you can do that for a few of the kids, consider your work a success. I like to set the intention that one person will experience awareness and be helped by the practice; that way I can usually be an overachiever. Even with kids who are rolling their eyes, you can plant seeds that may blossom in time, if not on your timeline or in your lifetime! Being aware of our egos is critical. All we can do is create the conditions for mindfulness; if we take too much credit for the "success" or "failure" of the young minds who are learning, we are not modeling self-care or right view of the situation.

TIPS FOR LEADING GUIDED PRACTICES

Here are some ways to avoid the missteps new facilitators often make when leading practices, especially guided meditations:

Speed: Speaking too fast is a common mistake, but speaking too slow can put your audience to sleep. Pace yourself with your breath.

Volume: Be sure you are loud enough. If you are too relaxed or speak too softly, people in the back might not hear you.

Tone: A calm, confident, and assertive tone is ideal. Take care not to sound hypnotic or solemn.

Words: If the words of a practice script don't resonate for you, improvise with ones that fit you and your kids.

Creating Contemplative Space

You may find yourself teaching in someone else's space. If you are an outsider, remember that you are a guest and must be respectful. Say thank you and always ask before rearranging anything. If you haven't set up the space yourself, use what is already there.

If you are in a school and know the school well, you can make connections between mindfulness and other lessons the kids are studying by checking in with teachers. Can metaphors be pulled from astronomy charts on the wall? Can you tie information about mindfulness of body to an anatomical model in science lab? Using your hosts' material has the added bonus of ingratiating yourself with them. An empty room can even work as its own metaphor. The room may be stripped bare to withstand destruction; we empty our minds so as not to damage ourselves with destructive thoughts. Working with whatever is present builds the important skill of creative improvisation. We are also modeling the practice of accepting what is here and making meaning of our environment.

If you can, put mindfulness reminders in the space where your group regularly meets, or even around the entire building. Be sure that your meeting is always listed on the school, hospital, or clinic calendar.

If the person whose space you are using is present, invite them to participate. Don't just ally with the other adults; empower them to assist and even lead practice. Keep coming back and asking every time. Your confidence and consistency create a sense of security for the kids and adults alike. Even if they decline every time, keep asking. In your personal practice, you didn't give up the first time your mind wandered and left you with your chaotic thoughts. So don't give up the first time an adult wanders off and leaves you with their chaotic classroom.

Making your space sacred is an important, though challenging part of working in institutions. These days, I am fortunate to have my own teaching space, but it was not always that way. When I worked in inner-city schools, my colleagues and I conducted therapy just about anywhere, including backstage in the auditorium, a storage closet, the top landing of a stairwell, and—no, I'm not kidding—a bathroom that had been converted into a supply room. Teachers, janitors, and other kids regularly interrupted our sessions. That didn't discourage my colleagues, who brightened up these otherwise dull therapy spaces with fresh paint and decorations to make them sacred for everyone. Do what you can with whatever space you're given.

If you do have your own space try to make it sacred, or at least special. I fill mine with things that symbolize important people and events in my life. Mementos from my favorite places, family furniture, and books I cherish are all around me. I look across my grandparents' carpet to see photos of my travels framing my patient's chair, and I see books by favorite teachers alongside objects that remind me of my mentors. You can liven up a space with inspiring quotes or poetry, brought in by you or by others. To give the kids you're working with a sense of ownership, ask them to bring objects that remind them of mindfulness and place them in the space.

Even in your own space, there may be limitations. Maybe the most you can do is create a mindfulness corner. If there isn't space even for that, then just a photograph, a poster, a bell, or a splash of paint can be your anchor, reminding and inspiring you and everyone who enters your space or walks past.

If you are teaching a group, you might want to think about how the children are seated. There is a range of opinions about sitting kids in circles versus rows; to me, this is a matter of knowing your kids. Does your group get silly and set one another off, or can they compliment each other and engage in discussion? Will your kids feel more self-conscious in a circle, or safer with everyone in sight?

If you are in an institution or school, what's the larger culture? Get to know the other adults, and cultivate allies and sources. Knowing the dynamics of the group is vital, so ask staff members about its emotional pulse, or have someone with you who knows its relational dynamics. They can tell you who should or should not be seated near whom, either for support or for safety.

Consider whether there is a certain time of day, or a context, in which kids are most open to new ideas and have a healthy attention span. Meeting regularly, on a particular day and at a certain time, and preferably when hearts and minds are most likely to be open, will make the experience feel predictable and safe for the kids.

When You Encounter Resistance

Encountering resistance, active or passive, is tough. The key, as in our own mindfulness practice, is to not take resistance personally. The best teachers in the world cannot get through perfectly to every student. So, go easy on the kids and on yourself.

Some forms of resistance are informative. Falling asleep is common among beginners, and I often joke: "We've been practicing for only five minutes, and you've already learned something—that you need more sleep! How can you get yourself the rest you need?" Giggles are also common, and you can draw attention to them as sounds or as a reaction to new experiences. I smile in acknowledgment but with a seriousness in my face as well—a look many parents and teachers have mastered. Kids may exaggerate the sound of their breath, or a certain movement. Sometimes they're being silly, but sometimes the exaggeration makes it easier for them to focus on the chosen anchor, so consider how you respond.

If a kid is really resisting a particular practice, there may be a good reason, and a different practice may be better. Some kids struggle to sit still, so asking them to play another role during a practice may be helpful. It may seem counterintuitive to offer the squirming kid the opportunity to be the bell ringer or the timekeeper, but they may rise to the occasion and, as a result, not disrupt the group.

Remember that while resistance can be frustrating, it is how we grow. A colleague pointed out that resisting gravity by learning balance is how babies learn to walk. Resistance offers you an opportunity to learn and do something differently the next time. Also remember that the more you cultivate clear-headedness with your own practice, the more able you will be to respond skillfully to a resistant kid, rather than becoming overwhelmed.

As you finish a longer practice, check if anyone is drifting off to sleep and needs a more direct reminder to come back. For example, if you've had the kids focused on an inner anchor, such as the breath, you might encourage them to bring their awareness outside, to the body as a whole or to the room. If you've had them focused on a sense, ask them to tune in the rest of their senses one at a time, wiggle their toes, or follow the sound of the chime until it fades, then have them open their eyes. I also like to remind kids that they are clearing a path back to how they felt in the practice, and that they can return to their mindfulness at any time through the breath, sound, body, or whatever anchor we just used.

If the resistance becomes too discouraging, or you veer into burn-out, take a step or two back, as suggested by the list on page 189, lean on your community for support, or check in with your own teacher and deepen your own practice.

After Practice: Leading Discussion

Skillful inquiry and reflection after a practice can help kids discover how mindfulness is useful in their lives. Allowing kids to discover the benefits for themselves, rather than telling them the benefits, is an example of teaching by showing rather than telling, and allows them to make mindfulness their own.

We can encourage kids to discover insights by reporting back on their practice and discussing their experience with adults and peers. Help kids put their insights to use in real life by making real-world connections to times and ways they used their mindfulness.

The kind of questions we ask and the direction in which we take a discussion may depend on our role: therapist, parent or teacher. Remember that every experience is valid, and we can validate the child's experience—positive, negative, or neutral—regardless of whether we think a practice "worked" or not. The more accepting we are with kids and their experience, the more open they will be with us and one another. Open, connected, compassionate curiosity is the best stance for helping kids feel heard and seen.

Processing, whether it's through specific questions, open discussion, or a moment of quiet writing or drawing, will help kids synthesize the experience and internalize the insights of the practice. It also empowers them by offering them a voice. If they struggle to express themselves aloud, you might encourage them to think, draw, move, or write. My collaborator and co-teacher Joan Klagsbrun says, "I'd like to hear what that experience was like for you—in a sound, words, images, movement, sensation, or however you would like to express it." In a group, we can ask kids to listen to each person, then reflect back what they've heard, giving everyone a chance to share.

A group discussion may not be best for all kids, so you might break it into smaller groups or pairs for reflection. Consider what form the sharing and discussion should take—open discussion, facilitated discussion, or maybe having one speaker at a time hold a talking stick or stone.

Avoid leading questions, but encourage discussion. Some people will like a given practice, and some won't, but they will all likely be quiet at first. Beginners in mindfulness practice tend to feel insecure and might ask, "Was I doing it right?" Remind the kids that there is no right or wrong and normalize their experience. Normalizing questions like, "Did anyone else's mind wander?" or "Did anyone wonder if they were doing it right? That's very common," are helpful. You can set the tone by sharing common beginners' experiences, maybe even your own beginning experience.

Asking younger kids about their experience is challenging, because, developmentally, they generally don't do well with open-ended questions. But we can still ask for specifics in open ways. Rather than the therapist's classic, "How did that make you feel?" we might ask, "How did you feel in your body and in your mind?" or, "What did you notice? Did you notice anything different from how you usually eat (or breathe, or walk)? What surprised you? Have you felt similar to that before? How did paying attention to a certain thing or in a certain way affect your experience? What did you like?" Don't be afraid to ask, "What did you not like?" or even "Any haters in the crowd today?" If a kid volunteers that they were bored or hated the practice, ask them to describe that feeling more deeply: "How did you know you were bored? What was boredom—a sensation in your body or thoughts in your mind? What did hating it make you want to do instead?"

The kids' reflections can give us a lot of information. Therapists half-joke that everything is diagnostic. Well, it is and it isn't, but everything can certainly be useful. When kids say they feel like they are doing a practice wrong, that opens the door to a conversation about how we judge ourselves and where that pressure and those voices come from. It also tells us something about how they feel about themselves. When they mention like or dislike, we learn about how they deal with discomfort or pleasure in the moment. In the discussion, we can connect the microcosm of the practice with how they deal with larger, real-life situations.

Our job includes giving positive feedback and praise, and both are most powerful when specific and immediate right after a practice. We can thank the kids for being open and for creating and sharing a space of stillness. When you catch kids being mindful and compassionate in their daily lives, name it for them and others, draw attention to it, and reinforce it.

You can also follow up by asking when kids used their mindfulness in the last day or last week. This positive behavioral support and reinforcement is far more effective at changing and reinforcing behavior than criticism or guilt. Shifting the praise-to-criticism ratio doesn't come naturally to all of us, and the more stressed we are, the more likely we are to nag about the negative rather than praise the positive. That's one more reason to renew your own practice: so that you can be mindful enough to recognize what's working well. You can also encourage kids to teach mindfulness to their friends and family. At the end of a therapy session, for example, I typically bring in the parent and ask the kid to teach the parent what we did that day.

Sharing from Your Own Experience

Part of considering how to get kids to open up is considering how much we want to open up ourselves. Sam Himelstein talks often about skillful self-disclosure as a mindfulness facilitator. We want to encourage kids' natural curiosity, but they may ask personal questions which we don't know how best to answer. Personal comfort, and our role in relation to the kids, will dictate what is appropriate to share. If you are a parent, you will likely share a lot. Teachers will share less. And many therapists are trained to disclose nothing about themselves. What is the balance between your role in the child's life, your personal comfort, and the safety and comfort of the kids? You need to know before you teach, or you may be surprised by how quickly your buttons are pressed and you reveal personal information without realizing it.

Questions to consider when we're disclosing information about ourselves include: What is my intention in sharing this? Is what I'm about to say in these kids' best interest? Is sharing this more about *me* or about *them?* Am I projecting something onto them? What are the potential consequences both long- and short-term of sharing this?

I have noticed that I share more in a group or school setting than I do as a one-on-one therapist, but as a therapist, I share enough so that kids know I'm human and that I've struggled with and benefited from these practices. Modeling comfort with our own imperfections offers kids a valuable lesson, but this does not mean being self-deprecating. Kids learn from our behavior, as well as our speech; we don't want to model putting ourselves down.

In the end, it's not about you and your experience—it's about their experience. The most important thing is to have an idea about what boundaries are comfortable and appropriate for you.

A Note on Trauma and Vulnerable Kids

For some kids, mindfulness practice can bring up a lot of stuff—good stuff, but also scary stuff. This also happens when a close relationship forms between teacher and student.

The good news is that stuff coming up is a sign that you are probably doing something right. Still, it may be overwhelming for both of you, especially if you're not working with your own children, or you aren't trained in mental health or trauma. Know and recognize your limits and the limits of your training. If you're a teacher, don't try to be a therapist, and vice versa; if you're a therapist, don't practice outside the bounds of your training or comfort. Seek help, support, and supervision when things get challenging. Always know your personal and professional boundaries, and also know your ethical and legal obligations for mandated reporting if a kid shares about abuse or neglect. Don't try to handle hard situations yourself, and never promise to keep a secret if you can't.

If you are teaching kids who aren't yours, especially vulnerable kids, the support of a community and close collaboration with other professionals is essential. Find out all you can about the kids' triggers, and who you, or they, can consult if their problems are beyond your scope. Mindfulness can trigger strong reactions: that's why it works and why it can be dangerous. As with medicine, the right dose is powerfully healing, but too much too fast can be hard on vulnerable kids. Know what you are doing, know your kids, and know your professional supports as much as you can.

It has been said that growth happens only outside of your comfort zone. I think it is more accurate to say that growth happens in the area between your comfort zone and your safety zone. So, we need to identify both the comfort zone and the safety zone for ourselves, and for the kids.

In the end, no book, workshop, or certificate program can offer the perfect advice for every moment of crisis in your life and in the lives of the children you're working with. No curriculum or technique will save you. As Vinny Ferraro from the Mindful Schools program says, "The curriculum is way down the list of what you have to offer." The best recourse in a challenging moment is you: your wisdom and your compassion—which will be more available to you if you yourself practice.

CHAPTER 13

enlightened community

creating a culture
of mindfulness

This is the real secret of life—to be completely engaged
with what you are doing in the here and now.
And instead of calling it work, realize that it is play.

ALAN WATTS, *The Essence of Alan Watts*

∪

You may, like many people, find yourself inspired to create a larger culture of mindfulness in your workplace, family, or larger community.

As mentioned earlier, Thich Nhat Hanh suggests that teaching children mindfulness is like planting seeds. If we follow this metaphor further, we can think of families as soil, schools as sunlight, and other institutions and adults in the community as the rainwater and fertilizer that will create the conditions under which mindfulness practice is most likely to grow and blossom. Even with all of these in place, we still cannot be certain a practice will bloom, but we do know that without them, we can be nearly certain it will wither.

A larger group that cultivates a culture of mindfulness is what Buddhists call a *sangha*. Having a practice community supports children, supports adults, and supports you. A strong community creates a sustainable, self-reinforcing contemplative culture that enables everyone's practice to thrive. This can be many things, especially in our increasingly secular society, where spiritual institutions are less and less the center of community. In their place, a family, a classroom, a school, a clinic, a congregation, a yoga studio, a community center, or something larger often becomes the default center of community. This group is the container that holds and allows the practice of mindfulness to flourish in the child, sustaining them through the challenging times, as an ecosystem nourishes individual life.

When we advocate for change in our children's schools or other institutions, there are unique opportunities but also unique forms of resistance. No one approach will magically create a mindful and compassionate community, just as no one practice will work for every child.

The intention of this chapter is to offer you some best practices for bringing mindfulness to your community, and is drawn from the experiences of parents and professionals who have been doing the work of creating mindful and compassionate ecosystems for years.

Considerations

When beginning any endeavor mindfully, it helps first to consider our intentions. Are they realistic, yet challenging? Other questions can help us reflect and then see a wise course of action.

Consider your role in the institution you want to work with or within. Are you an outside consultant (a role I often find myself in) or an insider, such as an administrator or employee? Are you a parent in a small family or an employee at a large hospital or school district?

What's your relationship to the kids? Are you a parent, a clinician, an educator, or something else?

Are you considering a top-down approach, in which a mindfulness program comes with a mandate from the leadership, or a grassroots approach, such as starting a small group of like-minded coworkers and growing the mindfulness from there? Are you using a curriculum, or improvising? Are you planning to go it alone, or to enlist colleagues or outside professionals? Who are your potential allies, and what are their different levels of knowledge, expertise, interest in, and skepticism about mindfulness?

When and how will the practice be taught: Each morning before breakfast? A one-time introduction at an all-school assembly? Through a therapy group? Will practice be integrated into every classroom, or as a component in health class or an after-school program? In a high-stakes-testing school, the best way to bring in mindfulness may be by integrating it into test preparation, when a few moments of mindfulness before an exam could substantially boost scores.

Getting in the Door and Making the Pitch

Approaching an institution from the outside with an offer to introduce mindfulness is usually an uphill climb. Public institutions typically have significant red tape and are wary of outsiders, and any organization that works with kids has safeguards in place for good reason: to guard the children's safety. With schools, you are probably better off being invited than offering services, unless you are already a parent or an experienced educator. However, institutions like libraries, juvenile prisons, community centers, after-school programs, or local spiritual communities may have an interest in offering free programming for young people. My friends at Wellness Works, a mindfulness organization in Pennsylvania, have had success by offering services to the most challenging (or perhaps, most challenged) kids. Another friend started volunteering at her children's school, moved on to the local library, and grew things from there. When the community sees the results, you'll almost certainly be invited back.

Engaging the adult gatekeepers is a challenge. Persuasion experts know that there are two routes: one through the head and one through the heart. You need to make both an intellectual and emotional argument for mindfulness and an experiential one. You may already intuitively know why mindfulness is important, but the research and theory given earlier in this book are there partly so that you can use them to persuade other adults. Your understanding can dispel myths and communicate the power of these practices in order to open minds, hearts, and doors.

The word *mindfulness* is trendy right now, and while we know mindfulness works by any name, we also know that everything changes and fads pass. Calling it mindfulness may actually give the practices a shorter shelf life than we would wish, so choose your words carefully. Terms such as *attention* or *awareness training, resilience, concentration, peak performance, enhancement,* or *optimization* might be preferable.

Most effective initiatives start with a workshop to orient parents, educators, staff, and other stakeholders before you begin working with the kids. Adults will need more than statistics, images of brain scans, and details about mindfulness programs for youth, although these certainly help. The more specific you can be about the return on investment—in terms of health and mental health, which are very costly, as well as grades, behavior, burnout (for staff and kids), staff turnover, or whatever terms are most relevant to the organization—the better. A recent study found that the best way to reduce restraints in a residential program was by training the staff in mindful stress reduction.[1]

More important than intellectual or emotional arguments is a direct and powerful experience of mindfulness that allows people to understand it on the gut level. As Maya Angelou said, "I've learned that people will forget what you said, people will forget what you did, but people will never forget how you made them feel." Mindfulness and compassion *feel good.* The shortest introduction I use is the four-part stress exercise described in chapter 1. This itself is often enough to convince skeptical adults of the value of mindfulness, especially if you ask how they would like their children to feel before those state exams or when renegotiating bedtime. Demonstrations also ease anxieties about mindfulness being religious in some way. Also, think back to what sparked *your* interest. Was it reading the research, experiencing mindfulness for yourself, or both?

The more other people get it, intellectually and intuitively, the more on board the rest of the family, school, clinic, or hospital staff is, and the more likely you are to see mindful awareness flourish in the rich fertilizer of community reinforcement. Offering a program first to the staff of an organization is an excellent way to build a foundation. This might mean advocating with leadership, human resources departments (many of which are already on board with mindfulness), unions, or the company health plan—all of which can save money on the health care and turnover costs that come from burnout. Funding may be tight for you, and part of your role may be finding creative ways to fundraise. But money is saved in the long run when staff performance and happiness improve. Many existing programs bring mindfulness to professionals for their own self-care; some are directed at teachers and therapists specifically. The parent–teacher association might contribute funding for joint workshops or mindfulness courses for parents and educators—a project I have been working on with a local hospital network. Most therapy and educational models that teach mindfulness to kids advocate that both the adults and the kids practice. Practicing mindfulness for themselves can make teachers, therapists, providers, and caregivers happier and better at their roles/jobs. Regardless of whether they share the practices with kids, they will enjoy the fruits of the practice. And when you are able to orient staff or parents to what you are doing, you will all speak a common language from a common experience.

Advocate that everyone in the community get some exposure to mindfulness, whether from a one-time talk or an ongoing group. Consider all the community stakeholders—not just the children and staff of an institution, but also the parents and alumni of schools, the boards of hospitals, the local corporate and private donors to clinics, and offer them an experience of mindfulness as well. School boards and even local politicians often have to at least humor you, as I found out when my friend Vanessa dragged me down to the statehouse to teach a few practices to our state representative. Parents and donors in some communities may be surprisingly generous once they understand and experience mindfulness for themselves. A friend of mine got a six-figure donation from a parent at his school who was in the parent mindfulness course. And don't forget, when offering a program to parents, to also offer mindful childcare.

You can also create a mindfulness resource corner or even a bookshelf somewhere at the organization. One colleague keeps a box of toys and props that can be used for practices, CDs and books on mindfulness, cushions and yoga mats, as well as binders of activities that anyone can easily find and use at her work station. As well as a resource box, it helps for an organization to have a mindfulness resource person, who can be a go-to for questions and a human reminder to the community just by walking around.

Where to begin to create culture change is a difficult question to answer. Most people who have found success agree that top-down approaches can result in more resistance than grassroots ones. Only in small institutions—such as charter and independent schools and small clinics or institutions with charismatic leadership—is this top-down change possible in the long term.

Better to start with yourself and a few other interested parents and colleagues and grow from there. Every organization has formal leaders and opinion leaders who hold power in different ways. A friend who works at Harvard Business School puts it this way: formal leaders are those who write the memos and policies; opinion leaders are who you go to and say, "What's the deal with the memo on this new policy?" The opinion leaders are the people you want to influence to create real change; they are the people you want to inspire with contemplative practice. These are the people who create the culture that trickles down. Wisdom from experts suggests that the best leaders are good listeners and consider themselves servants of the community rather than its masters.

Workplace interventions include advocating for (or offering) mindfulness to your fellow staff members or parents. Start a weekly meditation group, to meet during breaks or after hours once a week, or perhaps have the occasional mindful meal. From there, consider creating a mindfulness working group, study group, or practice group with interested community members. If you are in a leadership position, open and close staff meetings with short practices to integrate mindfulness into the week. Educate staff by holding mindfulness in-service trainings or paying for employees to receive outside training. Many communities do community-wide reading projects to anchor the year in a specific theme; consider suggesting a book on mindfulness. Share resources by making workshops, talks, and study groups open to everyone in the community, including parents, teachers, pediatricians, and other providers. Some of my colleagues have begun working at a local hospital to bring a day of mindfulness to all hospital staff, as well as the community the staff serves, at a few events a year.

A man I met recently in Finland started what is essentially a day of mindfulness in his small town. He calls it Do One Thing at a Time Day, and it is a day dedicated to practicing aspects of mindfulness. Winooski, Vermont, is trying to become the first mindful city. No doubt you can think of more approaches, small and large. In my conversations with people around the world, I see how much has blossomed from just a couple of interested individuals finding each other, sitting together, working together, and allowing their practice to spread to peers.

Chapter 11 discusses mindful moments in greater depth, and the practices in that chapter can be handy for connecting with other adults. Adults in even the busiest families and institutions *do* have moments here and there when they can check in with themselves, if they look for these moments. Twenty years ago, stressed-out workers found moments to breathe deliberately in the form of a cigarette break. Help colleagues find moments of peace in the busy day—that moment after the kids have departed for the next class, a one-minute pause between patients, or some other short space in the day. Just as small details can add up and overwhelm us, small mindful moments can add up and balance us out.

Whether your organization explicitly teaches mindfulness to children or not, the benefits of nourishing mindfulness in adults will affect everyone. If all else fails and resistance continues, compassion practices for the people in your workplace can inspire you, as can taking refuge in your mindfulness community, your own teacher, or your own practice.

Working With Institutional Resistance

Approaching coworkers or supervisors, especially as an outsider, can be far from easy, and you may encounter resistance. I recently heard

Vinny Ferraro ask a crowd of eager teachers whether they could recognize the difference between resistance and ambivalence. It's a question worth contemplating in your own practice, and it again points to the need for you to have a solid practice of your own, as well as an ally or two.

Resistance is usually based in fear, particularly fear of the unknown. *Institutional* resistance often arises in the form of legitimate fear about the very real limits on both time and money. Adding time for mindfulness is simple arithmetic, as it likely means taking away time from teachers or staff, potentially impacting test scores or other vital outcome measures. Fortunately, the evidence overwhelmingly shows long-term financial savings in staff health care costs and improvement in outcomes for the kids. When time is money, asking leaders to allot time for mindfulness to busy clinicians or teachers does cost something up front, but you can also show that with short practices, mindfulness doesn't have to take much time.

One insidious form of resistance comes from burned-out staff, which can be particularly difficult to counter if you are an outsider or in a management role. Burned-out staff may be understandably skeptical of the annual in-service training on "the next big thing." You can point out that mindfulness is an *old* thing that is becoming standard in education and healing, and that the organization is in danger of missing the boat on what leading institutions are doing. This may be the more motivating approach to opening minds, doors, and budgets. But remember that any time we challenge the status quo, people may take it personally, so making allies is critical. If we respect one another's wisdom and experience, we will have ready allies. If we challenge or talk down to people, we lose potential partners.

Twenty years ago in the psychotherapy world, mindfulness practices were considered fringe; they are now fully mainstream. To fail to recommend mindfulness for anxiety or depression is considered out of step with best practice. Most graduate schools in psychotherapy offer training in mindfulness for clinicians, and these are among the most popular courses. The same may soon be true for medical schools, nursing schools, education schools, and similar institutions.

In the child psychotherapy world, there's an adage that working with kids means working with families and larger systems and their respective constraints. Frustrating families, overworked social services providers, stressed-out staff—these are the unavoidable facts of working with young people. For many, myself included, this is where we feel most challenged. The kids I worked with in the inner city were often less challenging than the adults around them, whose resistance was contagious. Not only was the school itself intimidating, with metal detectors at the door and bars on the windows, but a corrosive cynicism pervaded the older staff, and I dreaded dealing with them.

One exhausted Friday afternoon, I plopped myself on my supervisor's couch. He could surely tell that I was at my wits' end, as I grumbled about what I perceived to be the stonewalling staff I encountered week after week as I tried to do something to help the kids. He sat back and indulged my rant for a few moments before stepping in.

"We are there to work with the kids. That's what we are contracted to do, and that's probably what you signed up to do," he explained.

I nodded in agreement and relief. Finally, it seemed like he got it. It was those *other* adults who were getting in the way.

Then he shifted in his seat. "But in reality, these kids are embedded in the world of the adults who surround them, embedded in the system. So what if, instead of trying to treat the kids and fight the system, you thought about your work as treating not just the kids but the entire system they are in, and seeing the kid as just a symptom of that larger sick system?"

This complex answer was not exactly what I wanted to hear that bleak winter Friday, but it did get me thinking. Over time, my supervisor's reply has become a refrain as I think about social justice in the larger picture. I still don't always know *how* to treat the system, but what he said helps me to approach my work in that larger way.

As the conversation with my supervisor continued, we spoke about the most frustrating staff members and remembered that they too were once kids and trainees. We discussed the stresses they were under and the fact that most of them had probably started off optimistic, if not idealistic, hopeful that they could be helpful. Over time, and with enough days like the one I had had, they had descended into bitterness. My own creeping cynicism was a red flag that something needed to shift—probably my own practice. Years later, it occurred to me that the only resistance I could do something about was my own.

So you may also wish to ask yourself, whose assumptions? Whose resistance? And also ask, who is suffering with this resistance?

Around this same time, my body was letting me know that I was getting burned out. Stomachaches and oversleeping plagued me on mornings that I went into one school in particular. You don't need to be a brilliant therapist to see the connection, but I was unaware of it until I reflected with peers and mentors. I deepened my practice and took a metta (lovingkindness) course at the local meditation center. My body began to heal, my heart reopened, and my reaction to the school shifted. There is an adage that pain times resistance equals suffering. Fighting resistance may lead you to more suffering. But I also offer another formula: resistance times compassion equals insight—insight into how better to deal with resistance.

Metta Practice

Consider doing the metta practice if your body, your mind, and your spirit (or maybe your partner, friends, and coworkers) are letting you know you are getting burned out.

Metta was developed specifically to deal with fear. The Buddha had sent his disciplines into the jungle, but they returned, afraid to practice alone where wild animals and dangerous bandits roamed. You and I may not be in the jungles of India staring down tigers, but perhaps you are staring down some tough students and staff in the concrete jungle, and fear and frustration have shaken your faith in yourself and your practice. Most spiritual traditions have some version of praying for your enemies or sending them kind wishes. Metta is a variation of that.

The process is simple. Begin by finding a comfortable meditation posture. It can help to place a hand, or both hands, over your heart, but this isn't necessary.

Begin by bringing to mind someone who only wants the best for you. We will call this person your benefactor. Perhaps this is an inspirational supervisor, an old professor, or another mentor. Perhaps this is someone who sparked your passion for your work when you were young yourself. Perhaps this is the person who first introduced you to meditation or to a spiritual path, or who inspired you to bridge your personal with your professional passions.

Now, make some good wishes for them—something like, "May you be happy, may you be safe, may you live in ease and at peace."

After a few days of doing this in your regular meditation practice, try to take their perspective, and imagine them sending such wishes to you. Or just make the same good wishes for yourself.

Notice that you are not saying you *are* happy, safe, or living in ease and at peace. But you are, like a kind friend, wishing that you will find and experience those things.

If those specific phrases do not speak to your heart and experience, find some that feel more authentic to you, and imagine hearing them from your benefactor. What words might they say to inspire you?

Perhaps: You deserve inspiration. May you find happiness and love. May you be fearless in your work to help others. May you be safe and secure in mind and body.

Spend a week of your regular meditation practice wishing these good things for yourself, perhaps viewing yourself from the perspective of this other wise person. For many of us, wishing good things for ourselves can feel uncomfortable, especially if you aren't used to receiving gratitude and kind wishes from yourself or people around you. But stick with it.

After a week, add in a colleague to whom it feels relatively easy to send such kind wishes, perhaps an ally in the system who encourages your positivity rather than your cynicism or frustration. Try integrating this into your regular practice for a week or so.

The next week, try bringing into your metta practice a person about whom you have no feelings, positive or negative. Maybe that secretary you see around but rarely interact with, or a janitor you don't speak to much.

The next week, begin sending good wishes to more difficult people in your workplace: a challenging parent, a tough administrator, maybe even a disruptive kid who gets under your skin.

Sending good wishes to difficult people is no easy feat, so start small and work your way up to them. "This is spiritual heavy lifting," I once heard teacher Noah Levine say. "That's why we start with the little dumbbells in our lives and then move on to the bigger ones!" If those big dumbbells are too hard, consider visualizing the person as an idealistic beginner at their work, or perhaps as a more innocent child. Or focus on one thing you like, or at least don't mind, about them. Wishing the best for others challenges our perspective, and if those difficult people were happy, were unafraid, were themselves and in touch with their original intentions and original goodness, their actions would be far different and less likely to trigger us. So, what better wish can we make for them?

Perhaps something mystical occurs when we say our chosen phrases, or perhaps our cognitive perspective is changed. Either way, your experience of the challenging people in your workplace is likely to shift. Even if they don't change, your reaction to them may. This means that wise and skillful ways to work with them will be far more likely to arise, because your mind is calm, compassionate, and open. The frustration about what they "should" do will dissipate. You may see your allies turn into friends, and once neutral parties turn into quiet sources of inspiration. Your "enemies" themselves may or may not change, but they can change from objects of frustration to reminders of something else.

Remember that these resistant gatekeepers are ultimately not the enemy. They are allies and teachers you haven't figured out how to use yet. Practice metta to open up new possibilities, but more importantly, to make time to act with compassion. Thich Nhat Hanh says that *compassion* is a verb. Live compassion in the real world, in the community around you. You are a beacon representing mindfulness and compassion. You can do formal practice such as metta, or you can just quietly support others. My friend Francis, for example, takes on a "secret mentee" each year, picking a younger staff member whom he deliberately takes time to check in with, offer support to, and just watch out for.

Working With Others

In organizations where there is competition for resources of time, attention, and money, it can be a challenge to remember we are all trying to serve the children; we just have different ideas about how to do that.

We all need clarity and humility in this journey, to remain open to new ideas and perspectives. Remember, we have much to learn from the people around us. Trust the therapist to do his job, the teacher to do hers, the parents to do theirs, and the other caregivers to do their best.

Also remember that we can learn from one another. As a parent, I learned more from friends and relatives than from any book I read on my own or in graduate school. As a therapist, I have learned far more about managing groups of children from teachers than I did in any group-therapy course. And I've learned more about human nature by people-watching in my travels around the world than from my education in psychology. This book is a distillation of the wisdom of those I've encountered in conversations, workshops, and books. Teachers, therapists, and parents can easily forget that they are working toward the same goals; it's wonderful when we can hold this is mind and support one another.

As you bring mindfulness to the community, you may be surprised by where you find and make allies. Be grateful for each one. Nurture and inspire one another regularly so that you have strength and support in the moments when you most need them.

In my quest to bring mindfulness to kids, I've found that one of the best ways to do that is by helping other adults. A cliché in helping professions reminds us that flight attendants instruct us to put on our own oxygen mask before assisting others. Self-care and our own practice is key to our efforts to share mindfulness, so make sure your colleagues know to breathe too. A few mindful staff truly living what they practice and preach, their actions and their presence informed by insights from their own practice, is a healing experience for most kids, whether or not you get around to explicitly teaching the kids mindfulness. A culture informed by the insights of mindfulness practice will make you and your colleagues the best teachers, therapists, caregivers, and parents you can be, exponentially increasing the chances of the kids flourishing.

By encouraging mindfulness among other adults in your community, you not only support your own efforts to help kids, but you also support them in their steps along your shared path of helping kids.

What can you do in the next week to contribute to a culture of mindfulness in your community?

IDEAS FOR CREATING A MINDFUL COMMUNITY

Keep attuned to recent events within the community.

Know the influential players—among the kids and among the adults.

Consider the merits and challenges of your role as an insider or an outsider.

Create a mindfulness sitting group or study group.

Consider a community read, community-wide trainings, or yearlong theme.

Bring all stakeholders—clinicians, educators, parents, staff—on board and offer them practice.

Hold a "Day of Mindfulness" or "One Thing at a Time Day."

Introduce a moment of contemplation at the start or end of meetings, whether it is a formal mindfulness practice or not.

conclusion

Grant yourself a moment of peace,
and you will understand
how foolishly you have scurried about.
Learn to be silent,
and you will notice that
you have talked too much.
Be kind,
and you will realize that
your judgment of others was too severe.
ANONYMOUS

I began trying to share mindfulness with kids in my early twenties. I was an idealistic, or perhaps arrogant, recent college graduate who thought he was going to change the world by teaching kids mindfulness. It was soon apparent that the students, not to mention the staff, at the therapeutic boarding school where I was teaching had other ideas. After I switched careers and began graduate school in clinical psychology, part of me thought that my career would consist of forty-minute meditation sessions with clients, with ten minutes at the end where we would discuss how much closer we were getting to enlightenment thanks to me. (I'm barely kidding, by the way.) My delusion was broken when a world-weary fifteen-year-old looked at me and, with a deep sigh and eyes rolling back into his head, said, "Dr. Willard, breathing is played out."

Creating and accepting new definitions of success has been one of the harder parts of the mindfulness journey for me. A mentor once told me, "In this work, we measure success with calipers, not yardsticks." He also helped me understand that progress is not always linear—something in-laws, insurance companies, and educational policymakers

don't always understand. I've learned that with some of the most troubled kids, our job sometimes is not pulling them out of a downward
slide or even stopping the downward slide, but just slowing the slide
and being with them when they are down. No matter how much you or
I think that the world's young people need mindfulness, they may not
be ready for it at this moment in their lives, no matter how fun we try
to make it or how hard we sell it to schools and institutions.

In these times, we are left with only one student whom we can
really influence: ourselves. Most of my best parenting, teaching, and
clinical work has come out of the insights, wisdom, and compassion
developed in my own practice and in my relationship with the kids I
work with, not in tools or techniques I've thrown at them.

It's now been a few years since I've worked as a therapist, and I still
don't get paid to sit and meditate for more than a few minutes out of my
fifty-minute sessions or the workshops I lead. I'm still not enlightened,
and frankly, those around me look a lot closer to enlightenment than
I do. My work looks different from what I envisioned long ago. Sometimes it looks like two people quietly practicing together. More often,
however, it looks like me trying to maintain and model mindfulness in
a room swirling with emotion. Your mileage may vary, as the commer-
cials say. In all likelihood, your practices with kids will look something
like what you've read in this book, but have a lot more of you, your
setting, and your kids in the words and in the implementation.

When I was practicing metta a few years ago, it occurred to me,
with a mixture of excitement and fear, that I might be a benefactor
in someone's life. We know that the best predictor of resilience in a
child's life is to have one adult who is there for them, who believes in
them unconditionally. For some child, that might be me. What a great
privilege—and a great responsibility.

Thich Nhat Hanh tells a story describing the importance of mindfulness in a traumatized community.

> In Vietnam there are many people, called boat people,
> who leave the country in small boats. Often the boats
> are caught in rough seas or storms, the people may

panic, and boats can sink. But if even one person aboard can remain calm, lucid, knowing what to do and what not to do, he or she can help the boat survive. His or her expression—face, voice—communicates clarity and calmness, and people have trust in that person. They will listen to what he or she says. One such person can save the lives of many.[1]

Are you willing to be that calm person in the boat with your kids—or with other kids in your kids' school, or in your workplace, your family, your community? If so, put down this book, come fully into the present moment with acceptance and nonjudgment, and begin from here.

May all beings be at peace.

notes

Introduction

1. Timothy D. Wilson et al., "Just Think: The Challenges of the Disengaged Mind," *Science* 345, no. 6192 (2014): 75–77.

Chapter 1: Stress and the American Kid

1. Britta Holzel et al., "Mindfulness Practice Leads to Increases in Regional Brain Gray Matter Density," *Psychiatry Research* 191, no. 1 (2011): 36–43. S. W. Lazar et al., "Meditation Experience Is Associated with Increased Cortical Thickness," *Neuroreport* 16 (2005): 1893–97.

2. David Black et al., "Notes from a Growing Science," and W. Britton and Arielle Sydnor, "Neurobiological Models of Meditation Practices: Implications for Applications with Youth," in *Teaching Mindfulness Skills to Kids and Teens*, edited by Christopher Willard and Amy Saltzman (New York: Guilford, 2015). Sara Lazar, "Neurobiology of Mindfulness," in *Mindfulness and Psychotherapy*, 2nd edition (New York: Guilford, 2013), 282–94.

3. Lisa S. Blackwell, Kali H. Trzesniewski, and Carol Sorich Dweck, "Implicit Theories of Intelligence Predict Achievement Across an Adolescent Transition: A Longitudinal Study and an Intervention," *Child Development* 78, no. 1 (2007): 246–63.

4. Sherry Turkle, "Connected, but Alone?", TED Talk, filmed February 2012. Available with interactive transcript at ted.com/talks.

5. Shunryu Suzuki, *Zen Mind, Beginner's Mind* (Boston: Shambhala, 2011).

Chapter 2: Mindfulness

1. M. A. Killingsworth and D. T. Gilbert, "A Wandering Mind Is an Unhappy Mind," *Science* 330, no. 6006 (2010): 932.
2. Carl Rogers, *The Carl Rogers Reader,* edited by Howard Kirschenbaum and Valerie Land Henderson (New York: Mariner, 1989), 19.
3. Susan Pollak, Thomas Pedulla, and Ronald Siegel, *Sitting Together: Essential Skills for Mindfulness-Based Psychotherapy* (New York: Guilford, 2014).
4. Lazar, "Neurobiology of Mindfulness."
5. Centers for Disease Control and Prevention, National Center for Injury Prevention and Control, "10 Leading Causes of Death by Age Group, United States—2013," graphic chart available at cdc.gov. Accessed August 13, 2015.

Chapter 3: Building the Foundation

1. Susan M. Bögels et al., "Mindful Parenting in Mental Health Care: Effects on Parental and Child Psychopathology, Parental Stress, Parenting, Coparenting, and Marital Functioning," *Mindfulness* 5, no. 5 (2014): 536–51.
2. Lisa Flook et al., "Mindfulness for Teachers: A Pilot Study to Assess Effects on Stress, Burnout, and Teaching Efficacy," *Mind, Brain, and Education* 7, no. 3 (2007): 182–95.
3. Ludwig Grepmair et al., "Promoting Mindfulness in Psychotherapists in Training Influences the Treatment Results of Their Patients: A Randomized, Double-Blind, Controlled Study," *Psychotherapy and Psychosomatics* 76, no. 6 (2007): 332–38.

Chapter 5: Visualizing Mindfulness

1. Elena Bodrova and Deborah Leong, *Tools of the Mind: The Vygotskian Approach to Early Childhood Education* (Englewood Cliffs, NJ: Merrill, 1996).

2. Simon Lacey, Randall Stilla, and K. Sathian, "Metaphorically Feeling: Comprehending Textural Metaphors Activates Somatosensory Cortex," *Brain and Language* 120, no. 3 (2012): 416–21.

3. Susan M. Orsillo and Lizabeth Roemer, *Mindfulness and Acceptance Based Behavioral Therapies in Practice* (New York: Guilford, 2009), 127.

4. Pollak, Pedulla, and Siegel, *Sitting Together.*

Chapter 6: Mind the Body

1. L. Nummenmaa et al., "Bodily Maps of Emotions," *Proceedings of the National Academy of Sciences* 111, no. 2 (2014): 646–51.

2. Mark Williams et al., *The Mindful Way through Depression: Freeing Yourself from Chronic Unhappiness* (New York: Guilford, 2007).

3. E. T. Gendlin, "Focusing," *Psychotherapy: Theory, Research and Practice* 6, no. 1 (1969): 4–15.

4. J. D. Creswell et al., "Neural Correlates of Dispositional Mindfulness During Affect Labeling," *Psychosomatic Medicine* 69, no. 6 (2007): 560–65.

5. W. Levinson et al., "Physician-Patient Communication: The Relationship with Malpractice Claims among Primary Care Physicians and Surgeons," *Journal of the American Medical Association* 277, no. 7 (1997): 553–69. John Mordechai Gottman and Nan Silver, *Why Marriages Succeed or Fail: What You Can Learn from the Breakthrough Research to Make Your Marriage Last* (New York: Simon & Schuster, 1994).

6. Jon Kabat-Zinn, *Full Catastrophe Living: Using the Wisdom of Your Body and Mind to Face Stress, Pain, and Illness* (New York: Dell, 1991), 92.

7. Thich Nhat Hanh, *Interbeing: Fourteen Guidelines for Engaged Buddhism* (Berkeley, CA: Parallax Press, 1998).

8. Brian Wansink, *Mindless Eating: Why We Eat More than We Think* (New York: Bantam, 2007), 73.

Chapter 7: Going with the Flow

1. John J. Ratey and Eric Hagerman, *Spark: The Revolutionary New Science of Exercise and the Brain* (New York: Little, Brown, 2008).
2. Richard Louv, *Last Child in the Woods: Saving Our Children from Nature-Deficit Disorder* (Chapel Hill, NC: Algonquin, 2005).
3. Jan Chozen Bays, *How to Train a Wild Elephant: And Other Adventures in Mindfulness* (Boston: Shambhala, 2011).
4. Fred Boyd Bryant and Joseph Veroff, *Savoring: A New Model of Positive Experience* (Mahwah, NJ: Lawrence Erlbaum Associates, 2007), 120.
5. Dana R. Carney, Amy J. C. Cuddy, and Andy J. Yap, "Power Posing: Brief Nonverbal Displays Affect Neuroendocrine Levels and Risk Tolerance," *Psychological Science* 21, no. 10 (October 2010): 1363–68.

Chapter 8: Shortcut to the Present

1. This quote appears in Stephen R. Covey's foreword to *Prisoners of Our Thoughts: Viktor Frankl's Principles for Discovering Meaning in Life and Work* (second edition) by Alex Pattakos, PhD, page viii.
2. Helen Keller, "Three Days to See," *Atlantic Monthly,* January 1933, 35–42.

Chapter 9: Playing Attention

1. Thich Nhat Hanh, *Being Peace,* revised edition (Berkeley, CA: Parallax Press, 2005).

2. Thich Nhat Hanh, *Planting Seeds: Practicing Mindfulness with Children* (Berkeley, CA: Parallax, 2011).

3. Adam Zeman et al., "By Heart: An fMRI Study of Brain Activation by Poetry and Prose," *Journal of Consciousness Studies* 20, no. 9 (2013): 132–58.

4. Simon Lacey, Randall Stilla, and K. Sathian, "Metaphorically Feeling: Comprehending Textural Metaphors Activates Somatosensory Cortex," *Brain and Language* 120, no. 3 (2012): 416–21.

5. Daniel Bowen, J. Greene, and B. Kisida, "Learning to Think Critically: A Visual Art Experiment," *Educational Researcher* 43, no. 1 (2014): 37–44.

Chapter 10: Making the Virtual Virtuous

1. Linda Stone, "Are You Breathing? Do You Have Email Apnea?" blog post, November 24, 2014. Available at lindastone.net. Accessed March 29, 2015.

2. Yalda T. Uhls et al., "Five Days at Outdoor Education Camp without Screens Improves Preteen Skills with Nonverbal Emotion Cues," *Computers in Human Behavior* 39 (2014): 387–92.

3. N. I. Eisenberger, "Broken Hearts and Broken Bones: A Neural Perspective on the Similarities between Social and Physical Pain," *Current Directions in Psychological Science* 21, no. 1 (2012): 42–47.

Chapter 11: Making Mindfulness Stick

1. Daniel Siegel, *Brainstorm: The Power and Purpose of the Teenage Brain* (New York: Tarcher/Penguin, 2013), 102.

2. Elisha Goldstein, *Uncovering Happiness* (New York: Atria, 2015), 72.

Chapter 13: Enlightened Community

1. Nirbhay N. Singh et al., "Mindful Staff Can Reduce the Use of Physical Restraints When Providing Care to Individuals with Intellectual Disabilities," *Journal of Applied Research in Intellectual Disabilities* 22, no. 2 (2009): 194–202.

Conclusion

1. Thich Nhat Hanh, *Essential Writings,* 162.

matching the practice
to the child

All practices given in the book are listed below. Some practices may be better for certain issues than others, though, in fact, most practices are good for most situations. To provide some guidance, I have noted when each practice might be most useful, using the key below.

There are no hard and fast rules, so please consider this only a guide, based on my experience and the experiences of other parents and child professionals. Feel free to adapt these practices to your kids. Many of the practices can also be found on my audio program *Practices for Growing Up Mindful* (Sounds True, 2016).

I = Introductory Practices. These practices are good for those taking their first steps in mindfulness practice, younger kids, or kids with short attention spans.

A = Anxiety. Practices recommended for anxiety quiet the fight-or-flight response. Many use the mind to reduce anxiety overall, while others bring awareness and relaxation to the body. Some cultivate a perspective beyond the anxious mind-set.

Breath practices are particularly tricky for those dealing with anxiety. When they work, which is most of the time, they work fast and effectively. But longer breath practices can make anxiety worse, since it's easy to feel that you're doing them wrong. Practicing these when anxiety is not present is key.

D = Depression. Most of these practices are "activating"—cognitively, emotionally, and physically—and therefore help lift us out of depressive rumination and learned helplessness. Some are grounding, which also helps us get out of rumination, and others bring in larger and more positive perspectives, which start to shift mood. Practices that are too relaxing may be pleasant introductions to mindfulness, but are not as helpful in the long run for depression.

F = Focus. These practices teach sustained and selective attention, sometimes in the face of distractions. They narrow the mind's focus, boost concentration skills, and strengthen executive function.

S = Stress / Burnout. Almost all the practices in this book are helpful for those suffering from stress. The specific practices identified by "S" help us recognize and get out of fight-or-flight or freeze responses, and re-regulate the nervous system. Some also help shift the mind away from a stress-based perspective.

T = Trauma. The most commonly used practices for those who have suffered trauma are grounding practices, which focus on external anchors through the five senses. I also include a few practices that teach awareness of trauma triggers, and some self-soothing practices.

It can be hard to predict whether a particular practice will be a challenge for someone who is dealing with trauma. Most of these practices are short and easy to do with eyes open. While visualizations can be helpful, I recommend establishing a base of positive mindfulness experience first.

PA = Performance Anxiety. These practices—recommended for those who find it hard to deal with situations such as tests, public speaking, sports, and social events—bring a focused awareness to how we feel, and quickly shift us into a more relaxed state.

R = Resilience. We all suffer setbacks and disappointments, but some of us find them particularly hard to deal with. The practices recommended for emotional resilience build self-esteem, self-compassion, and equanimity in the face of life's challenges and changes.

EI = Emotional Intelligence. The practices recommended to boost emotional intelligence help us recognize, tolerate, and work with our internal experience, and the ways in which the external world affects us.

ER = Emotional Regulation. These practices help us soothe challenging emotions, learn to calm ourselves, shift smoothly between emotional and cognitive states, and transition between different contexts. They are helpful in the face of strong emotional triggers.

IC = Impulse Control. The practices recommended for those who struggle to control their impulses teach awareness of triggers to action and skillful responses to inhibit triggers. Working with these practices builds patience. These practices are also useful for people struggling with issues such as cutting, aggression, and substance abuse.

Practices

3–2–1 Contact (p. 175): grounds and calms the mind and body. *I; A, F, PA, S, T*

7–11 Breath (p. 169): teaches deep breathing, and brings calm. *I; A, ER, S*

- **11–7 Breath** (p. 170): teaches deep breathing, raises energy and focus. *D*

Adapted Body Scan (p. 96): provides understanding of how emotions arise in the body. *I; A, D, EI, S*

Basic Mindfulness Meditation (p. 32): Offers an introductory lesson in how mindfulness works to shift our relationship to our thoughts and feelings, and how to stay present. This practice is good for everything.

Basic Walking Meditation (p. 108): provides an energetic boost (enables better focus than sitting). *A, D, PA, S, T*

- **5-4-3-2-1 Walking** (p. 114): brings attention and appreciation back to the senses and the world around us. *F, D, S*
- **Appreciative Walking** (p. 115): encourages a broader perspective. *I; A, D, EI, PA, R, S, T*
- **Penny Walking** (p. 115): narrows attention to movement, as well as the emotional experience of frustration. *I; F, IC*
- **Sensory Awareness Walking** (p. 114): brings attention from wandering thoughts and emotions into present moment senses and experiences. *F*
- **Silly Walking** (p. 113): helps get over self-consciousness and aids in transitions. *I; D, F, ER, IC*
- **Walking Characters** (p. 112): allows kids to "walk in someone else's shoes" and build empathy as well as awareness of how different emotional states may affect how they and their bodies respond to the world. *I; A, D, T, PA, R, EI, ER*
- **Walk This Way!** (p. 111): cultivates awareness of how body states affect mood. *I; A, D, EI, ER, PA, S, T*
- **Walking with Emotions** (p. 110): teaches awareness of emotional experience and mind-body connection. *I; A, D, PA, EI, IC*
- **Walking with Words** (p. 109): settles mind and body. *A, D, F, PA, R, S, T*

Breathing with All Our Senses (p. 171): teaches breath awareness and focus. *I; A, D, R, IC*

Butterfly Hug (p. 174): cultivates self-compassion. *I; A, D, S, T*

Clearing the Clouds (p. 138): accesses a greater range of emotions. *I; A, D, EI, F, IC, R, S, T*

Clouds in the Sky (p. 79): cultivates a larger perspective. *A, D, EI, ER, F, IC, R, S*

Color Detective (p. 181): trains attention and awareness. *I; F, PA, T*

Disappearing Sound (p. 122): grounds and calms the body and mind. *I; A, F, S, T*

Dr. Distracto (p. 133): teaches how to suppress impulses in the face of temptation and distraction. *IC*

Find the Song (p. 134): shifts and narrows attention. *F*

Five-Finger Breathing (p. 171): calms the nervous system in the mind and body. *I; A, ER, F, PA, R, S*

Four-Square Breath (p. 172): calms the nervous system in the mind and body. *I; A, S*

Glitter Jar (p. 83): creates comfort with changing emotions. *I; ER, IC, R*

Going with Your Gut (p. 53): tunes the mind in to the body's wisdom. *A, D, EI, R, S*

HALT (p. 176): teaches recognition of basic needs. *EI, IC*

How Do I Know? (p. 52): turns off the autopilot of rumination. *I; A, D, S*

Human Mirror (p. 135): teaches interpersonal and body awareness. *I; F, PA, EI, IC*
- **Human Kaleidoscope** (p. 136): group body mindfulness practice that teaches spatial awareness and interpersonal connection. *I; F, PA, EI, IC*

Ice, Ice Baby (p. 93): teaches tolerance of difficult emotions. *I; A, D, EI, ER, F, IC, S, T*

Just BE x 3 (p. 182): expands perspective. *A, D, PA, S, T*

Kind Wishes (p. 182): builds compassion and self-compassion. *D, T, R, EI*

Let the Music Move You (Emotionally) (p. 127): teaches recognition of emotions as they arise. *I; EI*

Metta Breath (p. 173): cultivates compassion for self. *A, D, EI, ER, PA, R, S, T*

Metta Practice (p. 212): cultivates compassion for self and others. *A, D, S, T*

Mind–Body Go! (p. 93): develops emotional awareness. *I; EI*

Mindful Coloring (p. 137): enhances focus, relaxation, and sensory awareness. *A, F, T*

Mindful Eating (p. 100): teaches healthy self-care and appreciation of the positive. *I; D, EI, F, IC*

More Than Words (p. 128): teaches recognition of emotional triggers. *EI*

Nagging Feeling (p. 179): teaches the ability to allow triggers or moods to pass. *A, D, EI, PA, S, T*

One-Track Mindfulness Practice (p. 127): grounds the mind and body. *I; A, F, PA, S*

Pass the Breath (p. 135): teaches how to slow down, take turns, suppress impulses. *F, IC*

Personal Space Practice (p. 95): develops emotional intelligence, personal comfort, and boundary setting. *I; EI, T*

SCANS Your Body (p. 179): teaches recognition of emotions as they arise in the body. *EI*

Seeing with Different Eyes (p. 181): perspective-shifting visual awareness practices. *I*
- **Artist's Eyes** (p. 182): shifts perspective. *A, D, F*
- **Child's Eyes** (p. 181): shifts perspective out of depressive mind-set. *D*
- **Samurai's Eyes** (p. 181): trains attention and awareness. *F*

Seeking Stillness (p. 177): grounds and calms the mind and body. *I; PA, S, T*

Sensation Countdown (p. 180): narrows focus and shifts attention. *F*

Sensory Scan (p. 174): builds body awareness and focuses attention. *I; A, F, EI*

Settling Practice (p. 86): grounds and calms the mind and body. *I; A, ER, F, R, S, T*

Seventy-Ninth Organ (p. 147): teaches awareness and tolerance of discomfort. *EI*

Shades of Green (p. 178): shifts perspective toward the positive. *I; A, D, S, T*

SIFTing Our Experience (p. 178): teaches recognition of thoughts and emotions. *EI, PA*

Silent Sigh (p. 170): releases negative and frustrated emotions. *I; A, D, F, PA, S*

Singletasking (p. 47): diverts attention from thought to the physical experience of the here and now. *I; A, D, ER, F, IC, PA, S, T*

SLOW Down (p. 176): relaxes body and mind. *A, PA, S*

Smile Meditation (p. 134): brings happiness and interpersonal awareness. *I; D, F, R, EI*

Social Media Mindfulness Practice (p. 155): counteracts unfavorable comparisons. *A, D, EI, S*

Sound Countdown (p. 180): narrows focus and grounds mind in the present moment. *I, A, F, PA, IC*

Soup Breathing (p. 168): calms the nervous system in the mind and body. *I; A, ER, PA, S*

Space Between (p. 173): narrows focus and trains attention. *F*

Stone in the Lake (p. 81): cultivates equanimity in the face of life's challenges. *A, D, ER, F, R, S*

STOP (p. 158): breaks the mind out of rumination. *I; A, D, EI, F, PA, S*

Surfing the Soundscape (p. 123): grounds and calms the body and mind. *A, EI, ER, F, PA, R, S, T*
   • **Dueling Sounds** (p. 124): narrows attention from many places down to a few, training selective attention. *I; A, F, IC*

THINK Before You Speak (p. 177): encourages reflection on speaking and helps manage impulses. *EI*

Tree Practice (p. 77): cultivates equanimity in the face of life's challenges. *A, D, ER, F, R, S*

What Went Well? (p. 52): shifts perspective toward the positive. *I; A, D, EI, R, S*

Write Your Own Mindful Breathing Meditation (p. 140): empowers kids in their own practice, offers a solid anchor and imagery for dealing with challenging emotions. *I; A, D, F, PA, S, T*

Zoom Lens and Wide Lens (p. 180): shifts attention. *F*

acknowledgments

This project feels more like an assembly than a creation; the words of wisdom, the practices, are more universal than my own. I have attempted to track down and give credit to everyone who inspired or contributed to any of them, but this is always a challenge in an oral tradition. So, thanks to everyone in the next paragraphs, and everyone whose name may not appear but whose spirit certainly appears in these pages.

First, I want to thank my wife, Olivia Weisser, who patiently listens to me ramble about my latest idea and then gives me the time and space to workshop it and write it. Being a writer requires sacrifice and support—not just our own, but that of the people who love writers as well! And, of course, thanks to my son, Leo! I also want to thank my parents, Ann and Norman Willard, for inspiring in me a love of mindfulness and a love of writing. Thank you also to my sister, Mara Willard, and her family.

My colleague Mitch Abblett read many drafts and offered many insights into writing, and has become, in other teaching and writing projects, the kind of collaborator that one dreams about. Other colleagues have become friends and supporters of this project by offering their feedback on chapters, including Mark Bertin, Geoff Brown, Fiona Jensen, Adria Kennedy, and Dzung Vo. Kristen Bettencourt helped greatly with feedback on various drafts and on the index—no small feat! Thanks also to Mark for the introduction to my agent, Carol Mann.

Many mentors have been there in moments of frustration and disappointment, to keep me going in my practices of sitting, psychotherapy, parenting, and writing, and their words also echo in these pages. Chris Germer, Susan Kaiser Greenland, Maddy Klyne, Susan Pollak, Jan Surrey, and Ed Yeats have been particularly inspirational as mentors, and to them I owe a deep bow of gratitude. Joan Klagsbrun, Tom

Pedulla, and Ron Siegel, along with the other members of the Institute for Meditation and Psychotherapy board, were also very supportive.

Many ideas emerged through conversations or talks I've heard. Only a few people I can recall to name: Chas DiCapua, Jeff Goding, Eddie Hauben, Brian Callahan, Ashley Sitkin, and others are responsible for many pieces of wisdom and practices in the book. Lee Guerette described the "swan and tiger energy." I initially thought that "Walk this Way" emerged from a conversation with a drama teacher, but I found a similar practice in Deb Schoeberlein's Mindful Teaching and Teaching Mindfulness. Sam Himelstein was incredibly generous in sharing his wisdom on how to approach challenging kids and was a strong presence in chapters 4 and 12. If you ever have a chance to attend a workshop with him, I can't recommend it highly enough. The community at the annual UCSD "Bridging" conference never fails to inspire me; conversations in hallways and over dinners with Steve Hickman and Alan Goldstein, Lisa Flook, Randye Semple, Meena Srinivasan, and others echo in these pages. I've absorbed wisdom from workshops by Mindful Schools with Vinny Ferraro, Megan Cowan, and Chris McKenna. Special thanks also to Vanessa Gobes, Francis Kolarik, and Peter Rosenmeir, who all appear in person and in spirit in these pages.

Thank you to my agent, Carol Mann, who connected me with Sounds True, a truly great publisher, and to Jennifer Brown and everyone in Sounds True acquisitions who supported the project. Thank you especially to Amy Rost, who steered me through the edits with insights I could never have found myself. Thanks also to Steve Lessard, who guided me through my first audio program, and my copyeditor, Allegra Huston, who shared wise insights as well.

Thanks so much to everyone who has ever attended a workshop with me or worked alongside me elsewhere: to colleagues at the Mindfulness in Education Network, the Institute for Meditation and Psychotherapy, and Zev Schuman-Olivier and everyone at the CHA Center for Mindfulness and Compassion.

Most of all, thank you to my child and adult patients over the years. It is for you that I write and teach.

index

about the author

Christopher Willard, PsyD, is a psychologist and educational consultant based in Boston, specializing in mindfulness with adolescents and young adults. He has been practicing meditation for over fifteen years. He currently serves on the board of directors at the Institute for Meditation and Psychotherapy and the Mindfulness in Education Network. Dr. Willard has published five books on contemplative practice. He teaches at Harvard Medical School and Lesley University, has consulted for dozens of schools and institutions, and has led workshops on four continents. His thoughts on mental health have appeared in articles in the *New York Times,* CNN (cnn.com), *ABC News* (abcnews.com), and elsewhere.

When not working, he enjoys spending time with his family, traveling, cooking, eating, reading, writing, and any combination of these he can manage.

For videos, downloads, and more information on workshops and training, including a list of mindfulness resources, visit drchristopherwillard.com. And be in touch on Facebook or Twitter.

about sounds true

Sounds True is a multimedia publisher whose mission is to inspire and support personal transformation and spiritual awakening. Founded in 1985 and located in Boulder, Colorado, we work with many of the leading spiritual teachers, thinkers, healers, and visionary artists of our time. We strive with every title to preserve the essential "living wisdom" of the author or artist. It is our goal to create products that not only provide information to a reader or listener, but that also embody the quality of a wisdom transmission.

For those seeking genuine transformation, Sounds True is your trusted partner. At SoundsTrue.com you will find a wealth of free resources to support your journey, including exclusive weekly audio interviews, free downloads, interactive learning tools, and other special savings on all our titles.

To learn more, please visit SoundsTrue.com/freegifts or call us toll-free at 800.333.9185.

sounds true
many voices, one journey